DIVORCE

TAKING THE HIGH ROAD

DIVORCE

TAKING THE HIGH ROAD

Simple Strategies for Creating a Healthy Divorce

Pegotty Cooper, CDC®
Kimberly Mishkin, CGRS, CDC®
Kira Wilson Gould, CDC®
Marc Levey, CDC®
Glenys Reeves, CDC®, MA, CEC, PCC
Lori A. Burton-Cluxton, MSW, CDC®
Pamela Y. Dykes, Ph.D., CDC®, ACC, MCM
Lisa M. McNally, CDC®
Marie Marhan Dropkin, CDC®
Tracy Callahan, MA, CDC®
Kurt B. Chacon, JD, CDC®

MOGULY MEDIA
Building Brands. Authoritatively.

ENDORSEMENTS

"So many clients arrive in my office believing their story demands they take revenge or seek "a pound of flesh" for what has been done to them. Witnessing their pain and watching the transformation to a new and often better life is a privilege that takes time and their best efforts. Divorce: Taking the High Road will allow them perspective upon why doing so is, in the long-term, much better for them and their children. The book is both about changing perspective, a mind shift, really, and changing the process too. Both components are clearly necessary to make divorce a more manageable and survivable experience."

Cherie D. Morris
CDC Certified Divorce Coach® / Life Transitions Coach
cherie@deardivorcecoach.com
www.deardivorcecoach.com

"This unique book exemplifies one of the very tenets of divorce coaching itself – to get multiple points of view! Contained in this book is the collective wisdom and approach of 10 different master coaches. Reading each section, each of which illuminates a key concept, you will actually feel as if you are being personally coached. Each coach generously shares his or her knowledge and approach in a way that you can instantly apply to yourself to gain new perspectives and make powerful choices through emotional mastery. I wish I could have read a book this authoritative and supportive when I was going through my divorce. It's a must-have now, for all of my clients."

Hanna Perlberger
Attorney, Mediator, CDC Certified Divorce Coach®

"I am looking forward to recommending this book to clients. It holds the potential to redefine how divorce is viewed, managed and experienced by everyone involved. This is a realistic and hopeful perspective for anyone who needs help and clarity to navigate an entirely new chapter in their life."

Ariane deBonvoisin
Author of "The First 30 Days", speaker, coach, entrepreneur
ariane@arianestudio.com

"With advice that is simple and yet has the power to transform a divorce into an empowering and revitalizing experience, this book shows us that a healthy divorce is achievable—and you don't have to do it alone! A must-read for anyone who is considering or is in the process of getting a divorce."

Stacy Francis CFP®, CDFA™, CES™
President & CEO of Francis Financial
http://francisfinancial.com
Founder of Savvy Ladies: http://www.savvyladies.org/about-us/our-story/

"Taking the high road in abnormal and often excruciatingly stressful circumstances is not easy. Stress alters who we are in the moment, and you might regret the things you say and do when you are in flight or fight mode, when you are "not yourself." When divorcing, that regret is amplified by the negative impact of your actions on your family, on your children. Read this book to discover how to be your best self in your divorce. I will be purchasing this book in bulk to hand out to my clients from now on."

Joryn Jenkins, Esq.
Collaborative Attorney, Trainer, and Author
Founder of Open Palm Law

"Everyone going through separation needs help. While people turn to lawyers and accountants, they most often need help from Coaches. Coaches serve an indispensable role in helping people stay focused during a tumultuous time in their lives where they are receiving opinions from multiple sources. Coaches help people sort through all the chatter and stay true to themselves and their goals."

Celene-Rose J. Polischuk, B.A., J.D.

Celene has been practicing law for 30 years with the majority of her practice being collaborative family law.

www.firststopfamilylaw.ca

"As someone who has experienced the trauma of separation and divorce I wish that there would have been a resource such as this and access to a coach who could have assisted me to remain my Best Self as I maneuvered through what at times seemed like an overwhelming process."

Kara Johnston, B.Com., MBA(c)
Survivor / Thriver of Separation and Divorce

"Divorce: Taking the High Road - Simple Strategies for Creating a Healthy Divorce is a valuable resource for anyone contemplating divorce. Each expert Divorce Coach contributor provides insights, advice, and examples of real divorce challenges to help readers understand the myriad of options available to them through the coaching process. The book addresses a broad range of issues with proven solutions to ease the way through and beyond divorce for the best outcome for all!"

Rosalind Sedacca, CLC
Divorce & Parenting Coach
Author & Founder, Child-Centered Divorce Network
www.ChildCenteredDivorce.com

"This book provides its reader with the unique opportunity to apply the expertise and wisdom of multiple professionals to help navigate through the life changing experience of divorce. With its focus on maintaining grace and dignity as one's family is restructured, rather than descending into bitterness and destruction, its authors offer much-needed perspective for those of us who feel we are traveling this difficult road alone."

Lorin Josephson
Registered Psychiatric Nurse, Professional Ethicist
Founder of "Philosophies for Living"
www.philosophiesforliving.strikingly.com
lorinjosephson1@mac.com

"In as much as divorce is one of the darkest times of anyone's life, the wisdom offered by the contributors to this anthology is a bright light that illuminates a healthy path through this challenging life transition. People prepare for a year or more to marry, six months or more to run a marathon, and train years to become experts in a professional field. Anyone would be well served by taking the time to prepare well for what is likely the most significant life transition they will ever experience and Divorce: Taking the High Road is a powerful tool for getting ready to 'un-marry' in a way that preserves dignity and well-being for everyone involved."

Adina T. Laver
Founder of Divorce Essentials
www.DivorceEssentials.net
Author: The Divorce Companion
www.DivorceCompanion.com

CONTENTS

Get 21 days of free support for taking the high road in divorce.

Visit www.highroadindivorce.com to sign up!

DEDICATION

To my partner, Randy Cooper, who makes it his ministry every day to help individuals and families to take the high road and has always believed that the divorce coach is the missing professional in divorce! (Pegotty Cooper)

For my beloved family. (Kira Wilson Gould)

To my beautiful children, Pearce, Darian and Addison, who inspire me each and every day to be the best that I can be. (Marc Levey)

To all who experience the transition of separation and divorce and work to remain their best-self. (Glenys Reeves)

I wait for the Lord; I wait, and put my hope in His word. ~Psalm 130:5 (Lori A. Burton-Cluxton)

I dedicate this chapter to my beautiful children. I take the high road for you. Braelen Brysen and Belicia. I give you all my Love! (Pamela Y. Dykes)

To the people I love and feel honored to have in my life...my parents - Anita & Leo; my children - Matthew, Meghan & Aiden; my grandchildren - Hailey, Aries, Adalyn, Aniah & Baby-to-Be; and my incredible husband - Jeremy McNally. (Lisa McNally)

Dedicated to all those dealing with a marital breakup. Like hell, when you're going though divorce, keep going 'til you're through it. (Marie Marhan Dropkin)

For Stephen, Conor and Mackenzie (Tracy Callahan)

For Isabella and Evan (Kurt B. Chacon)

ACKNOWLEDGEMENTS

Thank you to the following individuals who without their contributions, support and concept for this book, it would never have been produced.

Jeremy Kossen, our ever-inquisitive interviewer, is a professional writer and journalist. His advocacy and passion for collaborative divorce proved very effective in eliciting powerful insights from the professional contributors of this book.

Thanks also go out to Renee Harrison, our publisher and fearless project manager. Her organizational skills and positive attitude helped get all eleven co-authors through the often overwhelming and tedious process of content creation.

Jeremy and Renee are co-founders of www.Divorcebuddy.co and are on a quest to educate, empower and inspire couples to choose a more mindful and collaborative approach to divorce, and to always put the needs of kids first.

PREFACE

It is Mother's Day and one of my clients; let's call her "Carol," celebrated with her daughter, her husband and her ex-husband of now ten years, and her sister.

Several factors made this celebration today a milestone. Despite the fact that both parties in the divorce had agreed to mediation and not making it a contentious divorce, there were plenty of opportunities for veering off the high road.

Here are a few of the detours that were taken ten years ago:

- Carol's ex-husband had left her for another woman wanting to see if this relationship would work out before he decided if he wanted a divorce.

- Their daughter was very young at the time, and Carol confided in her how angry she was with her father for his irresponsible and cruel behavior.

- Carol refused to accept his terms and drew the boundary that if he pursued the other relationship, it would be as a divorced man.

- Carol's sister harbored resentment and anger towards her sister's husband because he had treated her sister with so little respect and had in essence also rejected the whole family.

- Carol's second husband, whose relationship with his own daughter had fallen apart due to parental alienation, found himself sometimes playing second fiddle to the dynamics of a daughter, ex-husband and the ex-husband's father who lived nearby.

It is never too late to take the high road…

Fast forward ten years:

- Father (ex-husband) and daughter have a close and supportive relationship.

- Husband and ex-husband share a bottle of expensive scotch enjoying the day and the company.

- Carol's sister and ex-husband exchange travel stories and information about unusual places they have visited.

And…

- Everyone participates in dinner preparation honoring the woman whose love they all share.

Families are complicated these days, and high conflict divorces tear apart not only families, but neighborhoods, communities, and multiple generations of relationships. Taking the high road means recognizing the need to preserve your dignity during the process, to develop at least working relationships to fulfill the conditions of the marital settlement agreement; and honoring the differences between you and your spouse so you can move into the next chapter of your life with your confidence and dignity intact.

Consequences of NOT Taking the High Road

But taking the high road and having a healthy divorce is easier said than done. Guilt and the other side of that coin, resentment, are powerful forces which cause unfortunate relationship damage not only within the nuclear family but also within the extended families.

Relationships that once revolved around the words "I love you" now convert the lovers into warriors fighting to the death, wielding these weapons in the most painful and public of ways! Social media allows people to vent and throw accusations around without having to be accountable to the person being accused. Taken to an extreme, intimate moments shared by two lovers can turn into revenge porn on social media, so the whole world gets to witness the relationship turned unto retaliation!

Children torn between two parents whom they love take the blame for the hostility and conflict. And their view of marriage could logically become: "Marriage? Never! Why would I?" Is it any wonder that so many men and women have children today without being married?

Want more proof of the devastating consequences when you choose not to take the high road and have a healthy divorce?

One of my Canadian colleagues Maria Manley shared this story she saw in the Toronto Sun in which an estranged wife became so consumed with jealousy, anger, and resentment upon discovering her husband, and the father of her only child was moving in with another woman. She ended up waging a divorce war that would last three years and cost the former spouses a combined $500,000 in legal fees.

Ontario Superior Court Justice Alex Pazaratz, who decided the case in January 2016, found the actions of the mother "unreasonable behavior," including her attempts to alienate the child from her father, "intolerable." The judge reproached her for "manipulating and falsifying evidence," for "provocative and dangerous behavior," that included "stalking" the father during pick-ups of the child. Also, he accused her of being "overt, manipulative, scheming, deceitful and oblivious to the needless family suffering she perpetuated for at least three years," and said this: "Our family court system has zero tolerance for this type of emotional abuse of children."

According to Pazaratz, "All of this could have been avoided. All of this should have been avoided. Courts have an obligation to deliver that message, so parents will stop pretending that hard-ball custody litigation is 'for the sake of the child.'"

Consequently, the mother was denied sole custody and ordered to pay $192,000 in costs to the father to offset his legal fees as she had repeatedly rejected her former husband's multiple offers to settle out-of-court and "ended up getting a deal far worse than those she rejected." (Michele Mandel, Toronto Sun, www.bit.ly/1XeSEo9)

Simple Strategies Provide the Fuel for the Journey

This book is divided into two parts: Part 1: Changing the Perspective, and Part 2: Changing the Process for Decision-Making.

Part 1: Changing the Perspective

The first section of the book provides you with some compelling examples of clients who have faced challenging obstacles and detours in taking the high road. Most importantly they had been willing to acknowledge the value of not doing divorce alone. They realized the power of tapping into the experience of others who could help them through the rough spots and realign their actions with who they know themselves to be when they are at their best, let's call this "Your Best Self."

Each chapter contains specific steps you can take in shifting your perspective so that you can make different choices and get different results.

Part 2: Changing the Process for Decision-Making

The second part of the book contains chapters which provide compelling reasons to explore the range of options for making decisions, negotiating the marital settlement agreement, and moving through the transition process to create the next chapter for yourself and your family.

In the chapters that follow – you will find simple strategies for dealing with frequently complex issues of divorce which often manifest themselves as destructive or disempowering emotional reactions – reactions which make it challenging to take the high road and create a healthy divorce. In such a state of mind, it is difficult to make the best decisions for your future.

Each of the chapters is derived from an interview with a high-integrity CDC Certified Divorce Coach®. Many of these highly-trained divorce professionals also represent other divorce professions such as therapy, family mediation or collaborative law. Each provides you with very specific actions that you can take which could result in your changing perspectives or changing processes which in turn could dramatically impact the outcome of your divorce process.

ABOUT PEGOTTY COOPER, CDC®

Pegotty Cooper is a Leadership, Career, and Divorce Coach in addition to being the Co-Founder of CDC Certified Divorce Coach® Program and co-author of the book: "Divorce: Overcome the Overwhelm and Avoid the Six Biggest Mistakes – Insights from Personal Divorce Coaches."

Practicing as a coach since 2002, Pegotty builds on a long career in management and executive leadership in helping people to recognize their strengths and to bring out the best in themselves and others with integrity, strong values and making decisions aligned with their best self.

A leader in the International Coach Federation and co-developer of the CDC College for Divorce Coaching® and the CDC Certified Divorce Coach® designation, Pegotty has experienced first-hand the transformational power of coaching to change the experience of divorce!

BUSINESS: CDC Certified Divorce Coach®

WEBSITE: www.CertifiedDivorceCoach.com

EMAIL: pegottyc@gmail.com

PHONE: 813.884.9511

LOCATION: Tampa, FL

FACEBOOK: www.facebook.com/CertifiedDivorceCoach

LINKEDIN: www.linkedin.com/in/pegottycooper

TWITTER: @DivorceCoachCrt

DIVORCE COACHING AS ACCESS TO TAKING THE HIGH ROAD

by **Pegotty Cooper,** CDC®

"Just as the 1990s brought the rise of life coaches, the new millennium is the age of the divorce coach." — *Geoff Williams, Reuters*

Personal Divorce Coaching: Making a Difference in a Process That Often Debilitates People for Years

Most people have a story about why they chose to become professionally involved with divorce – almost all of those stories derive from a very personal experience that they or someone close to them experienced. For me, I heard the commitment in my husband Randy's story about his parents' divorce and the impact it had on him. In his mid-life career expansion from CFP® to CDFA™ to Supreme Court of Florida Certified Family Mediator, he adopted divorce mediation and then divorce coaching as a way to help relieve children of the gut-wrenching experience of having family and friends torn from them as he had experienced as an adolescent. I also knew the shame from my early divorce which I hid for many years.

With seven years of experience behind me as a coach helping people through tough circumstances like workplace conflict, leadership challenges, performance issues and job loss, I knew that Randy would also be a great coach who could shine the light on the fears people had about money and finance. He has a way of simplifying very complex issues and helping people to wrap their arms around the process they need to follow one step at a time in order to arrive at a new approach to looking at an old problem.

When Randy completed his coach training, a lightbulb went on for him, and he could see that until then, the Personal Divorce Coach was the missing professional in divorce. Based on our work together in divorce starting when he became a mediator, we began to systematize and create a training program which we rolled out to our first class of the CDC Certified Divorce Coach® program in 2011. A few classes later we were interviewed by Geoff Williams, a writer for Reuters, who was writing an article about the emergence of divorce coaching. One of his quotes in that September 2012 article is "Just as the 1990s brought the rise of life coaches; the new millennium is the age of the divorce coach." In that article "What Can a Divorce Coach Do for You?" (Geoff Williams, Reuters, www.reut.rs/2aHewLD) he shared many perspectives on the value of divorce coaching.

You will also read other stories from 10 divorce coaches, each of whom is a CDC Certified Divorce Coach,® about how they came to this commitment called Personal Divorce Coaching.

What Exactly Does a Divorce Coach Do?

We have adapted the definition of divorce coaching, which appears on the American Bar Association (ABA) website as part of what we base our divorce coach training on:

"Divorce Coaching is a flexible, goal-oriented process designed to support, motivate, and guide people going through divorce to help them make the best possible decisions for their future, based on their particular interests, needs, and concerns. Divorce coaches have different professional backgrounds and are selected based on the specific needs of the clients."

And we add –

"Personal Divorce Coaching takes place where the rubber meets the road in the decisions, large and small, every day, which set the stage for creating the next chapter in the best way possible."

A Personal Divorce Coach supports the individual caught in the stress and overwhelm of divorce to keep moving forward towards that future one step at a time. To make the best decisions possible, a person experiencing divorce may need to increase the effectiveness of the tools they have at their disposal. In divorce, this is especially important when it comes to taking the high road and creating a healthy divorce.

Here is the framework that highlights the important actions which lay the foundation for taking the high road. All of the actions are connected to "Best Self" – that person you know yourself to be when you are at your best.

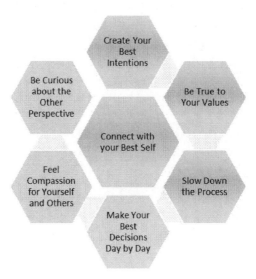

What Does "Taking the High Road" Mean?

"Taking the high road" means creating the best intentions for yourself and others who are impacted by your presence – be they family, friends, co-workers, people you do business with, neighbors, and anyone within your community circle.

It means retaining your dignity and preserving your self-esteem. And it means pushing through the times when you feel overwhelmed and hopeless by these circumstances which have the potential to turn anyone into someone they don't recognize.

It means choosing healthy boundaries, healthy practices, and healthy relationships even when you feel like doing just the opposite. In this way, you are modeling for yourself and others how to deal with challenging circumstances and be connected to who you are when you are at your best.

You Don't Have to Do This Alone!

While these may be simple strategies for taking the high road, the high road is not an easy one to stay on!

The whole landscape of divorce is filled with hazards which cause you to feel under attack and desperate to fight for your survival. There are changes at every turn in the road which you must deal with – from feeling isolated and alone to being out there on a limb financially with others relying on you for their survival. And the terrible feeling of not knowing how you are going to manage these changes without falling apart. And then there is the legal process with all of the unfamiliar rules and protocols and highly paid professionals who can't promise you anything!

A Personal Divorce Coach can be your thinking partner, your sounding board, and your champion to help you lay these foundations and be better able to take the effective actions you will need to be your best self and make the best possible decisions for your future based on your interest, needs, and concerns.

Some of the tools you will need for your journey on the high road include:

- Dealing effectively with conflict.

- Harnessing your emotions.

- Developing resilience.

- Being effective in two-way communication.

- Being a credible participant and client who is heard throughout the divorce process.

These tools are essential for every step in the process of divorce.

How is Your Decision-Making Impacted by Divorce?

Divorce overwhelms everything so it makes sense that it would also overwhelm decision-making.

The emotional roller-coaster of divorce, the multiple areas of change, and the often unfamiliar territory of the legal process of divorce can cause a drain on your decision-making capacity.

When the brain is impacted by sudden threats and chronic stress, chemical changes happen which are designed to keep you safe by activating your survival instincts – which usually involve fight, flight, and freeze. When your survival instincts take charge, the oldest part of your brain, known as the reptilian brain, takes over and the other parts of your brain, the creative and logical problem-solving parts, become disconnected. When your reptilian brain takes over, the emotional part of your brain, the amygdala, hijacks your ability to respond – and knee-jerk reactions happen in the blink of an eye. Good for survival in the wild – not useful for decision-making in divorce!

In these crucial moments – when you will be considering decisions which could have a significant impact on your future, and the sustainability of your family relationships – a divorce coach can help you to tame the reptilian brain and avoid some of the common pitfalls of decision-making.

Can a Divorce Coach Help No Matter What Process You Choose for Going Through Divorce?

While the choice of process is crucial – no matter what method for arriving at a divorce settlement you decide – there are ample opportunities to benefit from engaging a Personal Divorce Coach.

A Personal Divorce Coach can help you save money in the divorce process by helping you:

- Get organized for the process.

- Prepare for the meetings in advance.

- Think through what it is you want to get from the meeting.

- Acquire information you need.

- Be clear about what is important to you so that your attorney can make the case for that request.

Attorney Representation

Building a better relationship with all of the divorce professionals you work with by being a more credible client also helps you to be heard and to be a full participant in the process. This happens through aligning your expectations with what the attorney has agreed to provide; by being a better communicator about what is important to you and why; by letting go of the divorce story and being focused on the business of divorce; and being organized and responsive to attorney requests as you move through the process.

Legally Authorized Divorce Options

Collaborative Divorce

If one of you engaged in the process gets stuck and the process looks like it may derail, a Personal Divorce Coach can work one-on-one with one of the parties to help them see where their thinking may be hung up. Often a different perspective outside of the collaborative group can allow you to bring a new awareness to the discussion. In addition, lawyers are not trained as divorce coaches and do not have the breadth and depth of skills. And if they do, lawyers charge three to four times more than a divorce coach would to provide the same service. Mental Health Professionals (MHP) have many of the same skills, but in the collaborative process, the MHP is neutral. A divorce coach is a thinking advocate for you.

> *A divorce coach is a thinking advocate for you.*

Mediation

Perhaps one party knows what they want, and the other hasn't thought it through or there is a significant knowledge / understanding gap. Having a one-on-one thinking partner can help them to get educated, to fill in the missing pieces and to self-discover alternate options and a pathway to an agreement.

Pro-Se Divorce

A Personal Divorce Coach cannot provide legal advice as that is only the purview of a licensed attorney. But a Personal Divorce Coach can help someone think through what is most important, helping them to be open to listening to what is important to the other party in the divorce, and to find the common ground upon which to create agreement on how to split assets and debts. And a Personal Divorce Coach can refer each client to an attorney who is available just to review the agreement before filing with the court.

Personal Divorce Coaches Can Spot the Biggest Mistakes Before They Happen!

Overwhelm leads to serious decision-making mistakes in divorce which have long-term consequences for all parties involved. Everyone needs support in developing an awareness of their thinking so that they can weigh the decisions which have to be made and understand the consequences of those decisions as they go through the process of divorce and the process of transition from married to not-married. Many, if not most people, need support in keeping the overwhelm at bay and this means taming the reptilian part of the brain that out of necessity responds to threats quickly and precludes the slower more deliberate thought processes designed for creative problem solving from being engaged.

Here is the good news about the biggest mistakes people make in divorce – they are related to your thinking and perspective; your mindset, which you have the ability to change, thereby avoiding most of the legal and financial mistakes that are caused by this thinking. A CDC Certified Divorce Coach® is trained in recognizing these mindset mistakes before they result in irreversible decisions.

Where are the Breakdowns in Taking the High Road in the Divorce Process?

You have a hostile spouse who is not on that road…yet.

Even if your highest commitment is to take the high road and showing up as your best in the process, your spouse may need time to get to that place. If they have not initiated the divorce, they have started the process of adapting to this change at a different time – perhaps even several years later than you. You have already gone through the grieving process about the end of your marriage and all of the emotions related to that: denial, anxiety, shock, confusion and anger as noted in the illustration below. And now they need the time to go through the same process.

You are each in different places in the process of transition.

When change happens, it often occurs in an instant – circumstances change, a decision is made, something happens outside of us - and it sets in motion a whole series of adaptations that we have to make internally to adjust to that change. These are described in the work of William Bridges who has been working with this cycle of change and transition for the past forty years. His most recent book on the subject, "The Way of Transition", (www.amzn.to/2aBdVc1) is his journey through his own personal transition.

The process is one that moves from Endings, through a Neutral Zone where exploration can take place along with personal growth as you deal with the uncertainty of the in-between, and finally, you arrive at the New Beginnings. And you can see examples of the emotions and feelings you might have as you move through the process.

Each person goes through this process of transition starting at a different time, and also traveling at a different pace depending on so many different factors derived from personal history and experience, physical and spiritual well-being and general view of the world and change, among other considerations.

There are so many changes going on at the same time in divorce that you may have many of the transition processes overlapping. This can make it a process which also is not linear – there will be times when you are pulled back to a phase you have already been through because you may be impacted or triggered by another overlaying transition process. Be patient and remember you do not have to go through this alone!

There may be places where one of you gets triggered by a threat you perceive to be real even though it hasn't happened.

And this is where you get stuck and cannot let go and move on. You are holding on to an assumption or a belief that you aren't equipped to handle the decisions that need to be made, or you don't know how you will be able to survive on your own. Or you are unwilling to let go of old habits and ways of interacting with your spouse.

The ability to find greater purpose in your life beyond the divorce and to reconnect with your values, your strengths and who you are when you are at your best is how a divorce coach can support you as you move through the process of transition.

Here are some examples of how a Personal Divorce Coach works with someone as they go through this process:

Example 1:

Mary had been struggling to make the decision to divorce her husband for several years. They had been married for twenty-five years, and for the past ten years she had been miserable, and it was clear that they didn't see eye to eye on many of the decisions they made about finances, parenting, and lifestyle. And the bottom line was that Mary was having a hard time letting go of the marriage even though she filed for divorce. In working with the coach and identifying where her fear about the future was coming from, Mary gained clarity, confidence and some degree of certainty that things would be OK as she moved forward.

"My coach is a tremendous support and helped me see things more clearly and gain the insights I needed to move forward on my life journey."

Example 2:

Elaine came to me for coaching after her divorce was final. She was complaining about being overwhelmed and confused about her job and career direction. As we explored what she wanted moving forward, the divorce divorce and the past emotional abuse in the relationship kept coming up. Elaine had been working with a therapist and healing the wounds from a very domineering now ex-husband. But she was stuck and floundering in other areas of her life. One of the impacts was that she was afraid to make any decisions.

Since she had just moved into a new house, we explored some ways to celebrate and be kind to herself. The ideas included hanging up a few pictures in her new house so she would be surrounded by things that made her happy and enhanced her environment. The gift she gave to herself was the opportunity to make a decision without fear of the insults and criticism she had experienced during her marriage. This action was the thing that helped Elaine break through the fear of making decisions and be able to move forward with more decisions that helped her create her new life after divorce.

"I had an outstanding experience with my coach! She has helped me to set high goals (higher than I would have set by myself), my coach helped me to understand how and why I approach challenges and opportunities the way I do, and she helps me to reach the goals I've set."

Example 3:

Anita had been told by her husband of over thirty years that he wanted a divorce. When she came to me she was exhausted and feeling overwhelmed. Anita and her husband owned a business together, and she had always been the one to take care of all the operations in the company. She was under a lot of pressure to get this whole divorce project done.

Further examination of this revealed that she was the one putting the pressure on herself. There had not been any legal filing made, no legal process initiated, and no deadlines set. She was operating from habit and handling everything as urgent as she had in the business for several years. She was the one who could control the pace at which the divorce was moving forward.

When she saw that she had the choice to either drive herself to get everything in order OR to take care of herself and do some things she knew would be good for her heart and soul, she developed a new sense of freedom to choose. Anita could choose what would be most valuable to her based on a number of factors at the moment.

"I am so glad that you were the first person I talked with about my divorce. It was so helpful to get another perspective and to feel like I have the ability to decide what is best for me, including slowing the process of divorce down so that I can adapt to this new reality. I can work through my feelings of hurt, anger and sadness regarding the end of what I thought would be a life-long marriage. And I am now beginning to imagine some of the exciting things I can explore, things that engage my heart AND my head in ways I hadn't even been able to imagine earlier!"

What you can see in these stories is that a Personal Divorce Coach can help you:

1. Slow down – to change the pace of the process so that you can adapt to the new reality.

2. Identify small steps which can help you get unstuck and begin to move forward toward your new future.

3. Let go of old habits and redefine your future based on who YOU want to be.

And you will read more stories in the following chapters and get many more specific actionable steps that you can take in your desire to stay on the high road and create a healthy divorce.

How Do I Choose the Right Personal Divorce Coach for My Unique Situation?

As with all personal service relationships, you want to be sure there is a good match between you and the Personal Divorce Coach. Most offer a free consultation during which they will take the time to understand where you are now, what your goals are, what obstacles you are experiencing, and then identify how they can help you and what your divorce roadmap might look like.

You also want to be sure they have been specially trained to handle the unique aspects of the divorce process and that they have a Divorce Coaching Code of Ethics which they adhere to.

Also, ensure that they have a commitment to continuing education so that they are current with the tools and knowledge to best help individuals going through divorce. A Personal Divorce Coach needs to be equipped to deal with someone who may be on an emotional rollercoaster, who is operating from their most basic survival instincts, and dealing with an enormous magnitude of change with a legal process that they may be totally unfamiliar with.

Personal Divorce Coaches are also not bound to any one geographic area. They are free to practice without regard to state or provincial boundaries. Your choice of divorce coach may also depend on how you feel most comfortable engaging with your coach. Many hold sessions over the phone, some by Skype, Zoom, iPhone Facetime, or other video options; or they can meet with you face-to-face if they are located within a reasonable driving distance of your work or home.

P.S. Not Sure About Divorce?

Divorce Coaches can also help someone who hasn't yet decided to divorce and is grappling with the "Should I or shouldn't I?" question. They may be trying to understand the impact of divorce on all aspects of their life – approaching divorce from an "eyes wide open" standpoint to determine if the tradeoffs and consequences of divorce are the best decision for themselves and their family.

Personal Divorce Coaches do not advocate divorce, but if you find yourself in the situation where you need someone to help you through the rough spots in divorce, isn't it nice to know that you have a thinking partner and sounding board? You also have a champion who will partner with you to discover the best options for you; help you to learn new ways of looking at these overwhelming challenges, and rediscover who you are as you lay the foundations for your future.

The roll-up-your-sleeves kind of work that a divorce coach does helps their clients in ways that are different from a therapist, a mediator, and an attorney. A divorce coach complements these professionals' work in helping their clients make the best decisions for their future based on their wants, don't wants, and their needs. This work has a good chance of empowering them to take the high road and change their experience of divorce – for the sake of themselves and their family and their community!

For a list of coaches who hold the CDC Certified Divorce Coach® designation, go to the Find-A-Divorce-Coach Directory on our website: www.certifieddivorcecoach.com.

PART 1:
CHANGING THE
PERSPECTIVE

"Everything can be taken from a man but one thing: the last of human freedoms - to choose one's attitude in any given set of circumstances, to choose one's own way."
~Viktor E. Frankl

CHAPTER ONE

USING DIVORCE AS A CATALYST

FOR A BETTER LIFE

Interview with **Kimberly Mishkin**, CGRS®, CDC®

"Stepping onto a brand-new path is difficult, but not more difficult than remaining in a situation, which is not nurturing to the whole woman." — *Maya Angelou*

Jeremy: Kimberly, what inspired you to enter this field and become a divorce coach?

Kimberly: Like many divorce coaches, I went through a divorce. I left an abusive relationship after seventeen years. When I finally got up the courage to leave, I realized I didn't know what to do next. I didn't know anybody who had been through a divorce, so I just started looking up things online. I lived in New York City, and there I was, "Googling" attorneys. (I'm not exaggerating when I say I got twenty million hits.) I was operating in the dark, and I just wished there was somewhere to go for help with it all. I had endless questions, and at one point I was asking my attorney everything from legal issues to advice on how to pull myself together at work. It was the hardest time in my life, honestly. As I was going through it, I kept thinking, "There has to be a better way to do this. There has GOT to be a better way!"

A few years after my divorce, I had a challenging leadership job at The Spence School, and I loved it. But I was feeling the need to do something different, to give back somehow. As I talked with my family, they encouraged me to follow a dream I had mentioned, which was to help women go through divorce in a better, healthier way. I wanted to be "that place to go" that I couldn't find when I was going through my own divorce.

As I was thinking about this idea, I met Liza Caldwell, who is now my business partner and a good friend, volunteering in Léogâne, Haiti. As we talked and got to know each other, I found out that she, too, was divorced, and while her divorce circumstances were different from mine, she had the same experience. She muddled through her divorce too, without much support. When I met her, she had also been thinking about helping women find a better way to do this and envisioned a place where women could go to learn how to do everything – not only related to divorce but how to reinvent and start over fresh in their lives … a place where they could learn to use divorce as a catalyst for better living ultimately. It was fortuitous our paths crossed in Haiti because we decided to work together on our ideas. We opened our office in Midtown, New York in July of 2012. And ever since, we've been growing.

Jeremy: That's pretty interesting. You met in Haiti and later partnered. What are the types of people you help? Do you focus primarily on female clients?

Kimberly: Our company is SAS for Women® ("Support and Solutions" for Women.) We chose to work only with women because it's what we know best. Our work stems from our personal experiences, of course, but because we have a background in gender studies, we also know for a fact that women learn differently. We believe that men and women go through divorce very differently, too. We've always said that as our company grows, we will eventually open a men's division, but when we do, we will hire a very smart divorced man to run it. We feel like it is a different experience for men, and they deserve a coach who can relate to them specifically.

So far, our clients are women anywhere from in their thirties to sixties. They're educated — professionals or stay at home moms -- who come to us because divorce has thrown them for a loop. They don't know where to start. We know they need information; they need orientation, and they need guidance. We guide them through the logistics of the divorce and help them to understand that divorce is actually this incredible, open invitation to change the course of their lives … if they frame it the right way and if they do the work.

Jeremy: Women in their mid-thirties, or any age?

Kimberly: We've had a few clients in their twenties, but typically they are in their mid-thirties and up. More and more, we're seeing women who are coming to us after the kids have left for college. I just completed a year's journey with a wonderful client who was married for more than forty-eight years. She and her husband remain on good terms and are still friends. They just want to live going forward as individuals, doing different things, things each one of them has always wanted to do.

Jeremy: Can you walk us through what a typical coaching session would look like?

Kimberly: Sure. Let's start with the initial consultation. It's a free session where we get to know the client's story and we help her figure out what all she needs. Most important is that we help her identify ways that she might be able to take a step, even if it is a very small step, it is a step she can take *today*.

A client will come to us with a million things running through her mind. Maybe she needs to find a lawyer, or perhaps she's reached a sticking point with the lawyer she is working with. She may need to sell the house. She may need to move and has to find a place to live. She may want to know how to tell the kids about the divorce. Maybe she doesn't even know if she wants a divorce at all. It's all jumbled in her mind, and she is struggling to sort out her thoughts and to prioritize. Often, she'll come to us and spill her guts, and so we start there.

When you're in crisis mode, it all feels important. It all feels like it has to be dealt with right now, and the reality is certain things need to be prioritized. Our clients need a plan for how and when to get to everything. Much of what they need to do is very practical…they need to line up an attorney, gather financial information or do their taxes for the first time on their own. Perhaps they need to deal with the sale and packing up of the house or find a new apartment. We make a plan for those practical things.

However, there are also emotional things happening. Often they're very fragile. Their self-esteem may be very low… shattered even. They may be spent and exhausted and likely not taking care of themselves. They may be literally worrying themselves sick. It's certainly important to address all of the practical matters but it's equally, if not more important, to stop and address what's happening emotionally. We help them manage the stress and build a reserve of strength for the days when it feels like it's hard to get out of bed.

One of the biggest challenges during a divorce is the inability to imagine your life after the divorce is final. There are so many unknowns at first… you may not know where you will be living or where your kids will go to school next year… or you may be wondering if you'll have to go back to work and if so, what will you do? It's easy to get caught up in putting out fires and dealing with the immediate issues without giving much thought to where you will be in a year, or five or even ten years from now.

As coaches, we work with our clients to help them think bigger. We challenge them to be thoughtful about how they want to change and grow. There are unexpected gifts in divorce... a chance to learn from past mistakes, a reason to reinvent, an opportunity to create a life that isn't just a good life, but a GREAT one. It's great because you are conscious of every decision. You move forward with reasons. This turns out to be self-fulfilling. You move toward your goal because you are inspired. You are motivated. You reach your goal because you did the inspired work!

Jeremy: I know there are various challenges that women encounter. Maybe you could expand on some of the most common challenges or misconceptions that women have when they're going through the divorce process?

Kimberly: The biggest misconception, honestly, is that people think they have to do this alone. It's terribly isolating. Unfortunately, there is still shame associated with getting divorced. They may try to avoid telling their friends or family that this is happening, and that's the wrong way to approach it. You need not only to surround yourself with friends and family who love you, but you need a team of smart people who understand and have experience with divorce.

This is not the time to go it alone. You're not thinking clearly. When you're in turmoil, you're not able to access your logic and problem-solving abilities in the same way that you would if things were calm, on a normal day. This is the last time in your life that you want to try to be making big decisions in the dark and by yourself. Friends and family are critical, and they love you, and you need that.

However, friends and family aren't necessarily objective, so you also need pros. You need an attorney usually. You'll likely need a financial professional, and you need emotional support – like a therapist or a coach. I would make an argument that you need a divorce coach, somebody to help you coordinate all of what's going on for you. You need someone who can give you objective feedback and help you ask the right questions as you go forward and someone whom you'll feel safe with venting your rage, your tears, and your emotions. A divorce coach helps with all of the practical as well as the emotional aspects.

The biggest misconception that people have is they think they have to figure this out by themselves, and the reality is *they don't.*

ACT: Gain Clarity & Momentum

If you feel as if you are spinning endlessly, asking yourself, "Should I or Shouldn't I?" there are three things you can do that will stop the spinning and help you gain clarity and momentum toward a resolution. You must A C T:

Actively Seek Advisors

When you are in that place of confusion, a place where you can't see what's up or down, you need to talk with someone you can trust. We recommend a professional if possible. Whom you share with is important. What kind of professional?

- A therapist who will help you understand the emotional aspects

- A divorce coach who guides you through the whole process

- A lawyer who can talk to you about the legal journey

- The guidance counselor at your kid's school who has helped other families

What if you do not have access to a professional? Consider a friend, but first, ask yourself:

- Whom do I respect?

- Who will keep my story confidential?

- Who will give me genuine, constructive feedback?

- Who will suspend her/his own vested interests in my life?

- Who's been through the divorce process?

Collect Information

The unknown is the scariest part, so it's important to start gathering information. With the right information, you will make more informed choices, and you'll feel more in control of your situation.

- Find out what divorce laws are in your state

- Ask your friends if they have attorneys they would recommend

- Look for support groups in your area

- Look for free information: Go to workshops and attend webinars, sign up for free eBooks and newsletters and learn everything you can

Take a Step Everyday

Often we stall or avoid things that we really don't want to do or that are painful. This results in weeks and months slipping by without any progress. Instead, try to do one thing each day. Even if it's very small, take a step:

- Open a new bank account of your own
- Start a journal
- Make plans with a friend
- Schedule a meeting with an attorney or accountant
- Start looking online for a new house or apartment
- Reach out to someone you know who has been through a divorce

The key is to get out of your head and make a move, no matter how small. One step will lead to another, and you will begin to see and feel things differently. Tell yourself that taking action does not mean *you are necessarily* getting a divorce. It doesn't! It means you are finding out about your rights and your choices, and from there you will make the right decision.

Jeremy: I can understand that sense of shame, that feeling of "I have to go through this alone." That can be a huge challenge, and probably a misconception that I imagine the vast majority of people have at the very beginning.

How do you help your clients dispel that misconception and go through the divorce? You mentioned there were different support people, everything from the financial planner to the divorce coach. How do you help them and provide the support they need?

Kimberly: When clients come to us, they've often been living with indecision for a while. They know it's not working. They know they want things to change but they're not sure how to go about it, so there is a great deal of confusion and a whole lot of *fear.* Fear is the biggest thing they face in the beginning of the divorce process because they don't know what the future holds, and it all seems so scary. Sometimes women feel like they're going to walk away from a marriage and be homeless on the street. Money is a huge part of the fear factor. They also worry and wonder, "Will the kids be all right if I divorce?"

The first thing that we do is help women understand that they need to be in "information gathering mode," and that information will help to lessen the fear. Sometimes our fears are not based in reality. So, when working with women in this place, we start by looking at the real data. We look at their finances and help them start to make sense of the numbers. We connect them to vetted financial planners. We give them ideas about the legal process because they may not understand they have choices there. We educate them around the different ways to divorce and help them choose an attorney or the right means to seeking dissolution.

Clients come to us in the beginning scared and feeling like they're operating in the dark. Once we start putting some answers in place, we can make a plan and what's more, they start self-advocating more on their own. It's all about momentum and taking the first few baby steps, one thing at a time. Each day we try to accomplish something. They leave a session with us understanding what their next steps are.

Jeremy: Right. It's the fear of the unknown, and having that plan in place, or having some sort of certainty; that can alleviate a lot of stress.

Kimberly: Definitely. Also, we tell stories. There's comfort in knowing that you aren't the only one going through this. I give them examples of women who have done it before them, including my partner and myself. There is reassurance in having somebody hold your hand and knowing that she's done it before and that she knows where you are headed.

Jeremy: Could you tell me about a client who you've worked with who's gone through some difficult times? Maybe they were feeling alone, overwhelmed, but really through working with you, applying a lot of

these insights, they were able to emerge from the divorce in a place where they were happy and emotionally healthy?

Kimberly: Yes, absolutely. One, in particular, comes to mind, Jill. Jill came to me very distraught, in the middle of a custody battle that was headed to court, and she was frustrated with her attorney. She felt like it really wasn't going anywhere. Thousands of dollars had already been spent, and they were months into this process, but she didn't feel like anything had gotten done.

When I was listening to her, I didn't get the sense that the attorney was incompetent, but that my client really wasn't ... listening. She was too stressed. She wasn't able to absorb everything that was happening, and everything was feeling like an emergency.

I reached out to her attorney, with Jill's permission, and asked if I could attend the next meeting with them. In the meeting, it was very clear Jill was stressed to such a degree she couldn't hear what the attorney was saying, at all. I was able to calm her, to help her slow down and listen, and at times, translate legalese into simpler language so that she could understand what was being said. We had a great meeting, and the attorney invited me back, so I started attending meetings regularly as they were preparing for court. I helped Jill make sure we accomplished everything her attorney needed, like collecting and organizing documents and we rehearsed what she would say when it was her turn to testify in court. I even helped her shop for an outfit for court. She needed emotional support, first of all, but she also needed very practical support too.

This went on for a few months, and, in the end, the attorney invited me to sit in the back of the courtroom on the days that Jill had to testify. This was a huge shift for Jill. Just being able to look back and see me there calmed her. At the breaks, we would practice breathing exercises, and I would help her get her thoughts in order for the next set of questions that were coming up.

Outside of the courtroom, we were planning the next phase of her life. As I coached her, it became evident that she had a strong desire to go back to school and become a nurse, so we researched programs and she got into a good school. She was excited to think about becoming a financially independent woman, in a career that she actually loved. She was also very close with her young son and wanted to create a safe and serene home environment, something her son, unfortunately, had not really had up to that point. We talked about what that would look like and how Jill could create a loving and pleasant home life for her son, for them. I helped her realize that, even though things were a little muddy with the divorce *now,* ultimately she would be able to give her son the healthy and happy childhood he deserved for years to come.

Now I'm happy to report Jill is through her divorce and doing well. She came away from that crisis feeling like she wasn't doing it alone. She was bolstered. Somebody was there if she couldn't remember something or wasn't able to access a thought. I was her backup. She's in a much lighter, happier place now and has shifted her attention to being a single mom -- getting used to her new routine. I'm happy I was there to support her during a hard time, and now I'm there if she ever needs me for different challenges in the future. What we really do is help women using ongoing creative problem solving.

Jeremy: Do you work with clients when they already have an attorney, or before they've hired an attorney, or are considering collaborative law? Are you part of that process, in terms of guiding them on these types of divorce process decisions?

Kimberly: As a firm that advocates for women, we certainly try to steer our clients to "do divorce" the healthy way — avoiding court. Though sometimes litigation cannot be avoided, unfortunately. In truth, it's a small percentage of people who actually end up having a trial and a full battle in a courtroom. It's a very small percentage, and it should be, because it's destructive and very expensive.

More and more often our clients come to us at the beginning of the process, which is ideal for us, because (to answer your question) we do educate our clients about the different ways to get divorced.

We start by thinking about what process might be right for them, given their stories. When we talk about the options with clients, we describe it as a spectrum. At one end of the spectrum is the scenario of you, sitting with your spouse at the kitchen table and working out everything yourselves. At the opposite end of that spectrum are litigation and a trial where a judge decides everything for you because you were unable to negotiate a settlement, even with the aid of your attorneys. Usually, people fall somewhere in the middle, whether they use mediation, collaborative law, or each person gets his/her own attorney to negotiate a settlement with or for them.

Once we decide the right process, then we choose the right legal advisor, whether it's a mediator, a litigator, a family attorney, or a collaborative law team. We may or may not be involved in those meetings; that is up to the client. My partner and I both offer to accompany our clients to professional meetings. We're available to whatever degree that they need support. It depends on how triggered they are, how much stress they are managing, to what extent they feel like they can handle these things.

That being said, women come to us at all points in the process. I have a client who is actually well past her divorce, and now she's working to put her career back on track. I have another client who needs to revisit a custody agreement that's a few years old. But, more and more, clients are finding us at the beginning, which is great, because it means that they realize they don't have to go through this alone.

Jeremy: You made a good point regarding most cases, in general, they just don't go to trial. Taking an approach from the beginning that's less adversarial definitely makes a lot of sense.

Kimberly: Yes, especially if there are children involved. The last thing you want is a long drawn out, expensive legal battle, where you're pitted against each other because that's never good for the kids. Our message to clients is always, "How can you collaborate as much as possible?" This might be somebody you're going to have an ongoing co-parenting relationship with for years to come, so the healthier, less harmful path you can take, the better for everyone.

Jeremy: I was talking to somebody the other day about how marriage is like a merger, and a divorce is a dissolution. But, more accurately, divorce is more of a reorganization if there are children involved because there's going to be a relationship that exists for a long time.

Kimberly: Some clients tell me they don't know what to call their ex. I might suggest they say "the father of your kids" or your "co-parent". It seems like a simple thing, but it's big really. It's a paradigm shift that you're making, and while many couples wish they could just wash their hands and be done with each other, that's not the reality when you have kids.

We try really hard to help our clients keep things in perspective because this is not just for now. You're shifting to a new reality for as long as your kids are growing up.

If couples can manage to navigate the divorce with minimal negativity, they realize that this family reorganization is an opportunity to put the family back together in a way that is much healthier for everyone involved.

Jeremy: In closing, do you have any final words of advice? Are there any specific lessons or important things that you think people should consider?

Kimberly: I think I've made this point, but I think it's worth reiterating: Whether you are thinking about it or in the midst of it, divorce is not a time to try and figure out things all alone. It's too big. It's too important.

This is a time in your life for you to understand that you need real information. Don't stay in that place of wondering and worrying because you're scared. You don't know what will happen. You don't know what it will look like if you get divorced. The honest truth is, you don't know what you don't know, and that's okay.

Figure out which things scare you the most, and think about where you can gather information about them. Information will help you get clear; for example, what would it look like financially if you decided to make the choice to divorce? Get information from attorneys, line up free consultations, and use the many resources that are out there. At SAS, for example, we offer free consultations. We know what it was like to not know your path, which is why we do our best to make sure after talking with us, you have a mini-action plan to help you take one step that will empower you.

Finally, and most importantly, keep your heart and mind open to the gifts that divorce can bring. Think about what is vitally important to you and make sure those things exist in your post-divorce life. Don't let divorce define you. Use it as a vehicle to creating the life you have always deserved. When you do that, you will be amazed the places you will go!

Key Takeaways

√ **Actively Seek Advisors: Divorce is not a time to try and figure out things all alone, seek support.**

√ **Collect Information: Gathering information helps to alleviate fear.**

√ **Take a Step Every Day: Keep your heart and mind open to the gifts divorce can bring, use it as an opportunity to grow.**

9 Reasons to Hire a Divorce Coach

Ask yourself, are you experiencing any of the following? A coach understands these dilemmas and can help you take action to overcome them:

√ You are not thinking clearly

√ You are unfamiliar with the legal process

√ You can't get past your anger

√ You are paralyzed by fear

√ You either aren't making good decisions, or you aren't making *any* decisions

√ You don't understand anything about your finances

√ You don't know how to be a good parent right now

√ Your self-esteem is at an all-time low

√ You have no idea what you are going to do after the divorce is over

Your homework for today is to understand the more you learn, the more your fear will start to subside, and you will begin to understand what is true and what is not. Reading stories will help you.

Visit our website (www.sasforwomen.com) where you will find articles, checklists, videos, webinars, and events -- all kinds of resources to help you anywhere in the separation or divorce process, and life afterward. There are many other online resources for women and men where you can connect with people who have gone through or are going through divorce, too. Look for support groups or look on social media for daily inspiration feeds from leaders who motivate and empower you.

Whatever you do, get out of that place of shame and isolation! Start reaching out, start talking to people, start reading, start *connecting*.

SAS for Women® provides divorce support and coaching for women who are considering, in the process of, or recovering from divorce. Since our inception, we have helped women come to terms with questions such as what are the effects of divorce on children, how do I prepare for divorce in practical ways, and how do I deal with life after divorce? Our mission is to provide women comprehensive support as they navigate and grow from the process of major life-changes. We offer six free months of coaching delivered discretely to your inbox: www.sasforwomen.com/free-divorce-support-for-women *and complimentary consultations:* www.sasforwomen.com/schedule-an-appointment. *Connect with us to learn your next steps today: www.sasforwomen.com/contact-sas-for-women*

ABOUT KIMBERLY MISHKIN, CGRS®, CDC®

Kimberly Mishkin, cofounder, and director of SAS for Women®, is an educator of 21+ years and former administrator for The Spence School in New York City. Kim holds a BA in Education from Miami University, an MS in Science Education from Wright State University, and is licensed in Educational Leadership through The Ohio State University. She is a Certified Grief Recovery Specialist® with The Grief Recovery Institute® and a CDC Certified Divorce Coach®.

Kim left an abusive relationship after 13 years of marriage and is now happily remarried to a kind, loving, and generous man who taught her that marriage can be a wonderful partnership. She found the courage to make a big career change and after giving it much thought decided to use her experience to help other women navigate divorce and what can feel like, but doesn't have to be, a very lonely and confusing journey.

BUSINESS: SAS for Women®

WEBSITE: www.SASforWomen.com

EMAIL: kim@sasforwomen.com

PHONE: 646.438.5163

LOCATION: New York, NY

FACEBOOK: www.facebook.com/sasforwomen

LINKEDIN: www.linkedin.com/in/kimberlymishkin

TWITTER: @sasforwomen

INSTAGRAM: www.instagram.com/sasforwomen

CHAPTER TWO

SHIFT YOUR STORY – CHANGE YOUR LIFE

Interview with **Kira Wilson Gould,** CDC®

"Whatever words we utter should be chosen with care for people will hear them and be influenced by them for good or ill." — Buddha

Jeremy: Kira, you've done a lot of work helping people define their personal narrative, starting by ditching their old "divorce story." Before we get into the most important aspects of what a divorce story is and why it's important to create a positive story, can you share more about your personal background and what inspired you to help others as a divorce coach?

Kira: I came to this work the way a lot of us come to it, by experiencing divorce myself. I was a child of divorce, and I also experienced a divorce as an adult, one that was full of conflict and one that was not my choice. At least, that's how I viewed it at the time.

Through my divorce, I did a lot of soul searching. It's an opportunity to examine where you've been and where you want to go. During the process, which was full of tumultuous times and high emotions, I felt frustrated in that I didn't know whom to turn to exactly for help. I was one of the first of my friends to get divorced. I felt alone a lot of the time and overwhelmed by the process of divorce, all the legal, financial and emotional aspects, as well as the myriad of changes that came into my life.

I also felt frustrated with the help that was available. It was as if I were reinventing the wheel. In the midst of all this craziness in my life, I had to search for the right people, and they were often hard to find. You have to interview lawyers, find a good therapist, and hire someone to help with your finances, such as a Certified Divorce Financial Analyst (CDFA). Everything seems to come crashing down on you at the same time.

On top of it all, I hired the wrong family law attorney. I found myself fighting with him; he wasn't the right fit. But he was one of the only ones I knew. It just made the process so much harder and once I got out of that and was down the road a bit — five years out from my divorce — I could look back and see clearly that it didn't have to be like that. I set about searching for a better way to go through divorce — a way that limits the suffering, the overwhelm, and the tumultuousness of it.

That's how I found divorce coaching and just knew this was my calling — to help other women navigate their divorces. I primarily work with women; I work with men too, but I'm especially drawn to women. I streamline the process, helping my clients regain their power so that they can feel centered and clear. I'm that support, that anchor, that voice which helps them know where to go for whatever they need. I'm their champion.

You mentioned divorce story; I place emphasis on life stories and story in general. In my past career, I did a tremendous amount of writing; I recognize and understand the power of words, both spoken and written. Stories hold a lot of sway over us as human beings. We grow up with fairy tales, bedtime stories, novels, magazines, blogs, television shows, and movies.

I think we all love a good narrative, and we relate to them. What we say, read, and hear have incredibly powerful consequences that most of us don't even realize. Stories of life and divorce fascinate me. We all have one, whether we've been married, separated, divorced, et cetera. We all have a story to tell, and the words we use both to ourselves and others profoundly shape our past, present, and future.

I like to help people shift their story. Shift their story and transform their life.

Jeremy: How would you define a divorce story and how could having one be problematic?

Kira: We all have a story to tell. Whether you're contemplating divorce (and that means your story might focus more on the shortcomings of your marriage), or, you're starting the process of divorce, or you've even made it to the other side — you may still be trying to make sense of the whole situation.

That divorce story is what we tell when someone asks us about our divorce (or sometimes in response to a simple "how are you?"). The story could be told in person, or even on social media.

Every divorce is different. Therefore, every divorce story is different. Each one is unique, like a fingerprint. I do tend to see themes that recur. Typically, the divorce story is how your ex has wronged you in some way. Whether that's cheating or abuse (either verbally, emotionally, or physically), or being left or abandoned, ignored, not loved; it's something that's been done to you. When we're asked, we typically rattle it off with feeling and emotion — listing all the wrongs that have happened or been done to us. Often these things are tragic, and they hurt deeply.

The divorce story is how he or she hurt you, why they left you, and it tends to be full of blame, victimization, and shame (sometimes shame on you, but mostly shame on them). It's a story with a lot of pain and suffering and often very little choice. These are things that were done to us.

There isn't a lot of taking ownership or responsibility. My clients — and I have been guilty of this as well — we have very good reasons for our divorce stories. They're all based on actual events. I had a story I clung to. You could not shake me from my divorce story; I was sure that it was the truth with a capital "T".

The stories are painful. They're filled with drama and violence; legal battles and broken families; abandonment, betrayal, and devastation. And like I said before, it appears as if there was no choice or it seems like we had no control over how any of it played out — in our mind, or in our stories.

Each and every time I would tell my story, I would feel that pain all over again. The brain triggers all those synapses to fire, and it's like the hurt, the heartache, and the intense tragedy is happening to you all over again.

Don't get me wrong. There are some healthy ways of telling divorce stories and healthy ways of getting them out. Some people enjoy hearing your divorce story. After all, divorce is no longer a taboo hush-hush subject that no one talks about. Today everyone has been touched by or talks about divorce. We read about it in magazines; it's so commonplace with more than 50% of marriages ending in divorce. These days, everyone fancies themselves as experts. They have access to books and everything online, and they'll offer you advice. During your divorce, you might attract a lot of these people, ones who like the drama and sensation; and they're going to get in the middle of it with you.

At the beginning of your divorce you might enjoy all of that attention, and the reactions you get from people. You may even need it or crave more of it -- the sympathy, compassion, and empathy. That can be healthy at the beginning, but it tends to feed the fire of your story. The story grows, and you get more entrenched in the details. You might even start to make things up because you're seeking that reaction.

You can get caught up in this spiral of attention and drama, and it momentarily feels good, but at the same time, your poor brain re-lives and re-feels everything that happened to you. It's not healthy; you end up wearing yourself out. You wear out your friends and your family. They've heard it too often. They can't go on that roller coaster with you time and time again. You might even find yourself overwhelming perfect strangers.

I had a client who told me she broke down and lost it in the grocery store when the checker simply asked, "How are you?" She launched right into her story, full of emotion and tears. Meanwhile, five people were waiting behind her in line. Your story can sabotage you, or even take over your life.

Jeremy: That's an excellent point. Instinctively we like to share all the negative things; we're not going to say, "Well, basically I did this, and I did that, and I contributed to the breakdown of our relationship." There's a lot of blame and not taking responsibility for one's contribution to the circumstances that led up to the divorce. Then in the process, you're re-traumatizing yourself by bringing up all these different negative emotions.

What would be an example of a negative story? You explained what one is, but briefly, describe an example of a negative story you've encountered?

Kira: Negative divorce stories are much longer than what I'm about to share, but these are just to give you an idea…

Negative Divorce Stories

- "My ex cheated on me!"

- "He was a terrible father/she was a terrible mother!"

- "He/she ran out on us, he's/she's no good!"

- "He doesn't pay us a cent in child support."

- "She's crazy!"

- "I don't know how I lived with him/her for so many years."

- "He/she stole the best years of my life."

- "I don't deserve what he/she did to me, neither do my children."

- "I don't know how we'll ever recover."

The real stories tend to go on and on, with universal themes running through them such as negativity, and blame — which holds people back and prevents them from moving on with their lives in a healthy way.

Jeremy: Why do people get stuck in their divorce story? At the core, what keeps people, and what prevents them from moving on?

Kira: There are many reasons why we get stuck in our stories. Our story gives us comfort. It's a familiar place to re-visit. Change can be difficult and scary, and it sometimes seems safer to just stay with what we know — even if it's painful. We feel better momentarily when we vilify that other person who has hurt us.

Human beings, and I certainly am guilty of this, love to be right. It makes us feel better. Especially, when told from that place of blame or shame — shame on them; and focusing on what they did wrong -- we believe that our story is the truth, it makes us feel right.

We fall prey to that idea that we live in a world of scarcity where we need to compete for limited resources, whether that's for a person's attention or love, or who's listening to our story. We don't want others to feel sympathetic or empathetic to our ex; we need all of their sympathy and empathy for ourselves. We think we're competing for these limited resources, so we have to win. The idea of divorce is very much, "us versus them." It's a plaintiff versus respondent. It's a battle from the beginning. We want to win, and we feel better when we make someone else lose.

It's easier to get sympathy for our cause when we craft a compelling story in which we skillfully play the victim. You need to remember that when you relive that story and all the details, you're feeling the pain with each retelling. Think of it as a wound. If you keep opening that wound, scratching that wound, you bleed all over again. The wound doesn't heal. It festers. It gets worse than before.

It's normal to tell your story or share what happened to you on some level. There's a healthy amount of talking about your divorce and feeling the feelings; processing them and getting the support that you need. Then being able to move on, but if you can't stop telling your story, you can't move on. If you have that continued need to look for a reaction, that's when you know you need help, because again, you're going to burn out your friends and family. You're going to make strangers uncomfortable. You're going to alienate co-workers, friends, and maybe even parents at your children's school. It's too much.

Jeremy: And, of course, we now live in a world dominated by social media, so there's always a temptation to share everything on Facebook or some other social media site.

How do you see social media fitting into this equation? What are some of the pitfalls or things people should avoid when it comes to using social media?

Kira: I want to caution everybody that when you're getting a divorce, social media can be potentially dangerous. Facebook is not an invitation to slam your ex in a public way. It's often the first place your ex's divorce attorney will go to look for evidence.

Assume everything you write on social media will be read by your ex, his or her lawyer, your employer, and maybe even your children. Your kids could see what you put up. So, if you can't imagine your children reading what you wrote, don't write it.

Not to mention that your "friends" on social media tend to be people you don't really know. Two-thirds of them are probably mere acquaintances. Nobody online needs to know about your dirty laundry. When you're online during your divorce, stick to short, positive or neutral updates. You don't need to reiterate all the bad things that have happened to you.

If you're having trouble limiting your usage, just get yourself off of social media. Don't do anything, because bad mouthing your ex, or stalking him/her (both of which are bad ideas) is just damaging for you. It's not healthy in any way.

Jeremy: We discussed how to identify the potential problems with clinging to a negative story. Share with us how to solve these issues. What does a "healthy" divorce story look like and why is it so important for people to develop one?

Kira: A healthy divorce story is one that's short, positive and doesn't reignite all your pain. I don't want you to make something up. When I work with clients, I encourage them to examine the truth of their situation and come up with something that's honest and also healthy.

There are a variety of ways to shift your story from negative to positive. I like to work with each person by going into their story in a very intensive way. We don't like to spend a lot of time there because as I mentioned before, it's painful, and it reignites everything. We go in, and we pick out the parts of the story that are pertinent and really need looking at, shifting and re-framing. Then we take the troubling and negative aspects and transition them into how it can be a lesson, which once you learn the lesson, can lead to very positive experiences.

We want to explore what you learned from your marriage and your divorce because those lessons are incredibly expensive, and if you don't learn them, they come at way too high of a price. The lessons, they change you, they open you up to wonderful opportunities that allow you to do something else with your life. For example: "I learned x, y and z in my divorce, and that led me to become a better partner in my next relationship" Or "I've learned how to be more patient, compassionate and open-hearted."

After we do the exhaustive look, we can shorten the story from a narrative into a one- or two-line statement.

Divorce Story Statements

Some examples are:

- "We did the best we could given the circumstances."

- "We wanted different things out of life."

- "When one door closes, another one opens."

- "We wanted to move on and find partners who are better fits for each of us."

Ideally, it would be wonderful if you and ex are on the same page, and that you both basically say the same thing.

A lot of those examples I gave started with we or included "we" in it. Obviously, this is not always achievable. You can't control your ex or what he or she says, but for better or for worse, your lives are going to remain entwined for the sake of your children and the people you both know. Delivering a united message can be a huge relief to everyone.

It can be something that's neutral and definitely encompasses the truth. I don't want my clients to fabricate anything. There's always a way to shift and re-frame something from a negative into something that's neutral or a positive. It's just a matter of getting to that perspective.

Also, it's imperative to present a united front to one audience in particular, and that is your children. I can't stress this enough: tell them a similar story, or better yet, the same story. While you're getting divorced or your relationship is ending, put your vitriolic feelings aside, and sit down all together in the same room and communicate with an open heart.

You need to reassure them together how you're still going to be their mother and father. Even though the family will look different, you'll still be family. More importantly, you need to say that you both love them, and it's not their fault. Presenting a unified message that you share with your children will help them not to be confused. They do not want to hear one thing from daddy and something else from mommy — that would cause them to be torn and conflicted. You want to have a united message as best you can. I recognize this can be difficult, but it's really the ideal thing for your kids.

Jeremy: Is there a process or a particular method you recommend to develop what you would consider a positive divorce story?

Define Your Current Divorce Story

Kira: The first thing to do is write down your divorce story as you see it right now, without any editing, without any filters; just sit down and write it out in one go as best you can. Write as if no one will ever read it (and indeed, no one has to). When you're done with the process of writing the story down, read it, analyze it, and after you're done, you can burn it, and just let it go, which is incredibly healing and cathartic.

Another option is to spend some time thinking about what you tell people when they ask you about your divorce or what happened to you.

- What do you say?

- What certain themes get replayed?

- Where are you in control of your story and where are you playing the victim? It's that whole us vs. them thing.

- What is your ex doing in your story?

- Can you humanize your ex when you're going through the story?

- Do you recognize him or her as a person?

- It is helpful to think of them as a person – someone who has needs and wants, just like you. Are you able to do that in your story?

Review your story and pick these details out:

- Where are you placing blame?

- Is there a way to then look at it from a different perspective?

- Is there a way where you can see, actually, "I did that. I can take responsibility for that," or "I see he or she arrived at that honestly. They had a difficult childhood or difficult upbringing." Just try to remember that nothing happens in a vacuum. Every relationship is like a dance; it takes at least two people to be in a relationship.

Most importantly when you're going through this, it's not easy; it is not easy to put your story down on paper or try to shift your perspective. These are big things that I'm asking you to do. You need to be gentle and kind to yourself and just move at your own pace.

When I work with my clients, and we take stock of the divorce story, we then go a little bit further. We do a lot of visualization exercises.

Divorce Story Visualization Exercises

- What do you want your divorce to look like?

- How do you want your divorce to go?

- Who do you want to be through this process?

- How do you want to show up for your children?

- How do you want your friends to see you?

- What are your hopes and dreams, now and in the future?

- What is your life going to look like?

As you answer these questions, it's helpful to have support. Again, this is difficult work, so I encourage you to evaluate your support system. Do you have someone who is in your life already who's open-hearted, patient and loving — who can just be with you and help you examine this story? Because if you're having trouble writing it, it's helpful to go to a close friend and ask:

- "What do I say a lot?"

- "How do I repeat myself?"

- "Where are the themes in my story?"

- "Where do I get stuck?

Choose this friend wisely. You want them to be someone who is gentle and kind, but also honest and direct. They should answer your questions, and hopefully, they'll deliver their responses with love because the goal is to learn the lessons from this. It's sometimes difficult to figure them out on your own.

Jeremy: I can see how these exercises can be very cathartic. Can you share an example of a client you worked with who got bogged down in that negative narrative; they had a negative mindset but through their work with you and this process, they were able to transform their personal narrative into something that is what you would consider a positive divorce story?

Kira: Most people come to me stuck in their stories. Being stuck is the norm, rather than the exception. One of my earliest clients was the inspiration for a lot of this work (in addition to my general fascination with stories) because she was really, really stuck. And, it took us awhile to move her through her story. We'll call her "Mary," which is obviously not her real name. Mary was a lovely, beautiful woman, inside and out, and she had come to her story really honestly. She met and married an older man when she was young. He had been married twice before, and he had also cheated twice before. Unsurprisingly, he ended up cheating again and leaving her.

There were many, many red flags along the way and she didn't pay attention. Mary signed a prenuptial agreement that she didn't read. She found herself at the end of the separation and divorce without any alimony or assets. She was depressed and distraught. She had exhausted most of her family and friends. Mary was a victim in many ways, but she didn't want to be.

Mary wished to break free of this story that was holding her hostage, and she aspired to stop continuously telling people about her ex and what he'd done to her. We went into her story; we worked together on looking at where she could take responsibility and learning what she could from her actions. Mary came to realize incredible things about herself and recognize that she hadn't paid attention to the flags and the signs. She hadn't thought about the prenuptial agreement or how it would affect her, should the relationship end.

We worked together to come up with some positives. What are the positives of being on your own? What are the positives about building your life and your career? We came up with this really fun project that she labeled the "divorce bucket list," where she listed all the things she was going to do to take care of herself and bring joy back into her life.

Mary wanted to own those parts of the story that were hers so that she wouldn't repeat them in future relationships. She came by her divorce story in a very honest way. Those things happened to her; they were traumatic when he cheated and divorced her, he took everything, and Mary felt angry and justifiably so. But she didn't want to stay in that painful place; she wanted to be free of that story and move on with her life.

Jeremy: How else did Mary benefit from letting go of her old story and starting anew with a "healthy" story?

Kira: The most important thing Mary learned is the incredibly powerful distinction of perspective. I have a short story that basically illustrates the power of perspectives:

> *At the beginning of the last century, a shoe manufacturer was looking to expand its markets, and it sent two representatives to Africa to conduct research and report back what each of them found.*
>
> *One representative telegraphed back, "Situation is hopeless, stop. No one here wears shoes."*
>
> *The second representative telegraphed back, "Land is an endless opportunity, stop. No one here wears shoes."*

I just love that story — because no one in Africa wore shoes, somebody thought it was a dire situation while the other thought it was a land of opportunity. Life is all about perspective.

Divorce can be an incredible opportunity, but it's hard to get your head around it at first. However, your greatest tragedy can turn into your greatest gift. With a bit of perseverance, I think that's what Mary learned.

We, humans, tend to vacillate between two different illusions; either we think that we're in control of absolutely everything, or we fear everything is completely out of our control. For most of us, we live under the first illusion until something tragic like divorce happens to us. Then life spins out of control, and we go from being "fully in control" to the illusion of being completely out of control (I call this the pendulum swing). I work with my clients to establish a healthier view of life — that it's partly within your control and partly out of your control.

I love the quote, "Life is 10% what happens to you and 90% how you react to it." Your reactions are potentially under your control, especially if you learn the skills to "respond" rather than "react." How beautiful and wonderful is it to know you can control nearly 90% of your life. That gives you an incredible amount of power. You can now create your story, create your life, and your new story can be one of possibility, opportunity, joy, and abundance.

Jeremy: That's an invaluable perspective, viewing a situation that may seem traumatic at the time as an opportunity; nearly every problem, every challenge, has a solution. Here's a solution that also presents an opportunity for growth. Too often we're inclined to attach to that negative story. How else do we benefit from ditching — or just letting go of the story?

Kira: We talked about ditching the story and developing a healthy one- two- line divorce response, and you don't need to stop there, right? Letting go of that story allows you the freedom to re-frame what your divorce means or meant. It puts you into that field of possibility where you can spend time dreaming about and then designing and reinventing your life.

Because divorce is an opportunity for transformation, I named my company, "Getting Unmarried," and the tagline is "Redefining Happily Ever After." It is a chance to rewrite your life and give yourself a starring role as the lead actor, director, producer, writer and maybe even the audience.

That may sound slightly narcissistic, but when you spend time getting in touch with who you are, at your very best, at your core, you're able to connect with your heart and your humanity, and ultimately reinvent your life from this place of deep connection. That can be incredibly healing and intensely powerful.

Like my clients, you too can stop living in the past. You can construct a life that you love to live. You can stop reliving the pain and the heartbreak of your divorce. You get to move to a place of forgiveness, joy, happiness, and eventually love — like love for yourself, your family, children, and also if you desire it, romantic love.

Jeremy: Kira, what do you see as some of the main advantages of working with a divorce coach to help you transform your divorce story?

Kira: I think a divorce coach can be an incredible advocate for you, a sounding board, someone who can help shift your perspective, celebrate and recognize the steps you've made along the way. They can be there to acknowledge all the progress and the things you've done that are worth recognizing because this is hard work. Especially shifting a story that you've been wedded to. When you want to make that transition, that shift, you need someone to help you.

Being supported in a way that is positive and constructive exponentially speeds up your healing process. The perspective you will gain can help you minimize certain aspects and keep things from getting to be completely overwhelming. There are so many details and changes that come with divorce. It's practically everything! It's your house, it's your finances, it's the shape of your family, your friends, and your career. It's the one thing in adult life that touches almost every aspect of the life you've created. Divorce shakes it up, and you don't want to experience that alone or with the wrong support. You need someone who can support you fully in all aspects, whether that's legal, emotional, or financial. You want that person who can guide you and walk with you the whole length of that journey.

Coaching is very different from family law. We look at the divorce in a holistic way and help you become the driver in your divorce — you should be the one controlling your divorce, including the legal, healing, emotional, and financial aspects. You should be the one deciding on how it's all handled and whether your divorce is mediated or litigated, or if you just do it yourself. You should be the one holding the reins, and as a coach, we help you create the type of divorce you envision for yourself.

We help keep YOU in charge, not the attorney, not the therapist, and not the financial planner. The attorney's job is to get you divorced, and have it finalized. They're not necessarily there to help you feel better. Their job is to dissolve the marriage. The divorce coach is an expert to help you throughout the whole process. We help you minimize the overwhelming confusion; we support you in everything that you're going to face in your divorce.

Key Takeaways

√   **Words have the power to hold us hostage and stuck in our divorce pain, or the ability to set us free and on a path to create our new life.**

√   **The typical divorce story is one full of blame, shame, and how someone wronged you in some way; you are the victim.**

√   **There are healthy ways to shift your divorce story; the first step is being aware of what your story is, the second step is re-framing it into neutral or positive language.**

√   **Edit yourself in all ways of communication, but especially with what you say to your children, and what you put up on social media.**

√   **Support is key when changing perspectives. Lean on a trusted friend, family member or professional, who can help you see things in a different light.**

Kira is available through Facebook, LinkedIn, and Meetup. You can visit her website — www.getting-unmarried.com. Access valuable insights about the "getting unmarried" concept and how to "take the high road" in your divorce, your story and in your life. Download free PDFs with tips and exercises for writing and analyzing your divorce story. And if you'd like help shifting your story, Kira may be reached by phone at 310.963.9563.

ABOUT KIRA WILSON GOULD, CDC®

CDC Certified Divorce Coach® and certified real estate divorce specialist, Kira Gould is dedicated to helping people "get unmarried" in a conscious, clear and compassionate way. In addition to one-on-one coaching, real estate guidance, workshops, and retreats, she offers two free support groups: "Getting Unmarried: Women Reinventing Happily Ever After," and "Moving On: Divorce & Real Estate".

Kira is tied into an extensive network of divorce and financial professionals/ experts who support, protect, educate, and nurture her clients through this time of upheaval and change. Together with her team, Kira helps minimize the conflict, overwhelm and fighting, and maximize her client's well-being as well as their bottom line.

Kira works with clients during any stage of their divorce: from thinking about ending a marriage, in the process of divorce, or transitioning to life after the split. Her goal is to provide a supportive environment that helps her clients to move on, both literally and figuratively. She handles anything and everything related to divorce, including keeping the marital home, managing emotional ties, minimizing financial fallout, and effortlessly transitioning from married to happily single. Through Kira's guidance, her clients move on with hope and purpose.

BUSINESS: Getting Unmarried

WEBSITE: www.getting-unmarried.com

EMAIL: kira@getting-unmarried.com

PHONE: 310.963.9563

LOCATION: Los Angeles, CA

FACEBOOK: www.linkedin.com/in/kira-gould-118aab10

LINKEDIN: www.facebook.com/getting.unmarried

CHAPTER THREE

FIVE STEPS TO A MINDFUL DIVORCE

Interview with **Marc Levey**, CDC®

"To subdue your enemy without fighting is the supreme art of war." — Sun Tzu

Jeremy: Marc, those who know you, know that your approach to resolving conflict -- as well as your approach to life in general -- has a "Zen-like" feel to it. Can you share with us when and how you developed this style?

Marc: Growing up in a fast-paced city like Los Angeles, I was seeking balance in my life by the time I went to college. My studies focused on international business with a specialization in the language and culture of Japan.

My professors insisted that if I wanted to understand the mindset of the Japanese politician or businessperson, I would need to immerse myself not only in the history, art and literature of the people but also in the belief systems that influence each and every part of their daily lives.

Jeremy: How did you go about that process?

Marc: I spent a great deal of time learning about the principles of Buddhism, Taoism, and Confucianism. And it didn't take long for me to see how these practices had long-lasting, positive effects on my teachers: they each exhibited a powerful sense of balance and inner peace. And I say "powerful" because they were far from being weak or easily manipulated. On the contrary, these humble monks were anchored in a self-awareness that was unmistakable and they "said" a great deal by saying very few words at all. Coming from the United States, particularly Los Angeles, this concept was entirely different than what I grew up understanding.

Jeremy: Can you expound on the lessons you drew from Eastern principles?

Marc: From the start, I noticed that the concept consistent across each of these spiritual teachings was awareness, also referred to as "mindfulness." And since then, I've tried to apply the practice of mindfulness throughout my life, both personally and professionally. Over the years, I have found that during moments of intense conflict or disagreement, by being mindful, I was able to make more rational, less emotionally-charged decisions, which had a far more positive impact on my life than if I had reacted impulsively.

Once I started coaching individuals who were going through their own high-conflict situations -- like divorce -- I began to see how mindfulness could help my clients generate exceptional results from a place of calm, clarity, and confidence.

Jeremy: Mindfulness, particularly in divorce or other high-conflict situations, is a powerful concept that we often overlook. And, most people in North America, or the West, aren't typically familiar with the concept. We hear the term thrown around a lot, but to provide greater clarity on its meaning, can you delve deeper into what mindfulness is and how someone going through divorce can apply mindfulness to help them survive the process?

Marc: Mindfulness is a way of observing what's going on in your life, from a more relaxed and objective point of view. It doesn't eliminate life's pressures, but it does help us respond to them in a manner that's more balanced and open-minded. It gives us a bit of time and space to consider our options rather than acting out impulsively. It doesn't mean that you'll be immune to feeling emotions like anger, resentment, or jealousy; it does mean that you'll catch yourself feeling this way, call yourself out on it, and ideally, let the emotion pass by rather than react to it.

As you know, during a divorce, both parties are expected to make dozens, if not hundreds of life-altering decisions, for themselves, for their children, and even for their spouses. These decisions will have a profound impact on everyone involved for many years to come. And considering that divorce can be one of the most intense experiences in a person's life, not only legally and financially -- but also socially, emotionally, and spiritually -- it's easy to see why so few divorces end on a healthy note.

And I say, "healthy," because, in the end, when all the dust settles, isn't that what we really want for ourselves and for our families?

Thus, I've found that by helping clients take a moment to step back from the situation, assess their options, and contemplate their futures, they can approach the challenges and decisions of their divorces more strategically and less impulsively -- more logically and less irrationally.

Jeremy: It sounds easy enough -- so what do you think keeps most people from behaving this way on their own?

Marc: Aside from the obvious pain, frustration and anger often associated with couples going through a divorce, we've all been socialized to "win" rather than to collaborate.

Jeremy: We're clearly socialized to be highly competitive creatures. Why do you think this is the case?

Marc: We live in a society that is highly competitive, where from early childhood, we are bombarded by competition in school, sports, business, and politics.

Even though we, as a species, are driven forward by competition, it's the completely wrong mindset when entering Family Court, which is all about cooperation and collaboration.

The problem is that we're socialized to believe "that for one of us to win, the other must lose." We are accustomed to a win-lose paradigm.

While this may be the case on the football field, in Family Court, it doesn't work that way. With rare exception, there are either two winners or two losers.

Jeremy: Is this why you chose to work with highly competitive professionals?

Marc: Yes. I've found that highly competitive people like professional athletes and C-level executives often struggle with the concept of cooperating and collaborating with those who may be causing them pain and suffering. For someone who has succeeded in business and life due to competition, it's entirely counter-intuitive for them to look at divorce any differently. They don't understand how a trait that can make them so successful in other parts of their lives can be so detrimental in Family Court.

Therefore, it requires the establishment of a new mindset. One that focuses on REDEFINING, REFRAMING, and RESTRUCTURING elements of the divorce process.

Jeremy: Could you explain what you mean by Redefining, Reframing, and Restructuring?

Marc: In short, we start by…

REDEFINING the Divorce Process

Redefining what it truly means to "win." Contrary to popular belief, "winning" in life is far more complicated than "winning" on the basketball court or at the poker table. "Destroying" your spouse through divorce may feel like a "win," but I assure you it is a temporary "high," especially if you share children. Instead, we need to focus on what "winning" can feel like in the big picture and set our course accordingly.

REFRAMING the Divorce Process

We then work on **Reframing** many of the pre-conceived notions of divorce to lessen the suffering commonly associated with it.

RESTRUCTURING the Divorce Process

And finally, we work on **Restructuring** the family household in a way that can benefit the entire family rather than just one parent.

Jeremy: Can you share a real-life example of an exercise you use in your practice to help people implement this process?

Marc: Often, competitive people don't understand what it truly means to be a co-parent. An exercise I use with clients today was shared with me by my mentor years ago when I was going through my divorce:

My mentor asked, "What is the most important thing in your life?"

I answered, "My children."

He said, "Great. So, for purposes of this exercise, can we place a valuation of $100 billion dollars on them?"

I wasn't sure where he was going with this, but I agreed.

He said, "So you're the co-chairman of a $100-billion-dollar corporation."

Again, I went along with him.

And then he hit me with, "So guess who you're co-chairing this corporation with?"

I sat there in silence, letting the reality sink in.

He smiled and continued, "Just like in business, you don't have to like your co-chair, and you definitely don't have to love them, but you DO have to communicate with them if you want your venture, or your children, to succeed."

This simple exercise helped me reframe what co-parenting meant to me, and from that point on, I was able to remain laser-focused on my priorities as a father, and as a co-parent.

Jeremy: What a brilliant analogy. Now connecting this to Eastern philosophy, how do you believe the principles of divorce coaching are very much in alignment with key aspects of Buddhism, Taoism, and Confucianism?

Marc: Buddhism is all about creating balance in your life by seeking and maintaining a broad perspective.

Divorce coaching is all about managing a client's expectations by helping them step back and gain perspective by consulting with experts in various fields.

Confucius aspired to help people become the best possible versions of themselves through a set of principles, including living one's life with integrity and dignity, and staying true to one's personal values.

Similarly, your divorce coach is there to encourage you to resist getting pulled into the mud by your spouse. Instead, we support our clients to envision themselves at their very best and to act accordingly. If they are exhausted, we help them foster resilience and expand their capacity for patience.

Lao Tzu, the revered mystic who inspired Taoism, saw humanity and nature as one. He believed that those who recognize their innate connection with the whole would never act out of narrow self-interest.

Similarly, in divorce coaching we help our clients understand the impact of their decisions beyond themselves; how their actions will affect their children and others in their lives.

Jeremy: Who handles divorce better? Men or women?

Marc: The consensus is that divorce is tougher on men than women. In part, this is due to the fact that roughly 70 percent of divorces in the U.S. are initiated, or filed, by women. Being the non-initiator means that most men are taken by surprise, and are, therefore, in a state of shock that quickly turns into denial when they realize how seriously life is about to change for them and their families.

After their initial shock and denial, men typically get angry. Their anger is fueled by a sense of powerlessness brought on by a feeling of emasculation. Most find themselves stuck in a situation beyond their control. They feel like they are being dragged through the process of divorce by their spouse. They feel like everything is being taken away from them: their money, their homes, their kids, and even their social status, which may result in significant resentment, hostility, and even violence.

Jeremy: Can you share more on the differences between how initiators and non-initiators process divorce and how they may be affected differently?

Marc: There are two main points to remember when it comes to the initiator versus non-initiator. Regardless of gender, typically the initiator has started the process of transition much earlier than the non-initiator. Studies have shown that many who initiate divorce have been considering it for 6 to 24 months before filing for divorce. By having started the process much earlier, the initiator has had more time to contemplate the realities of divorce than the non-initiator, who must now play "catch up" once the divorce has been initiated.

It also means that at any given point during the divorce process, the two parties may be at very different places within the transition, and therefore, experiencing and exhibiting very different emotions and behaviors. This has a significant impact on how each party may perceive the other. For example, the initiator may appear to be a cold-hearted villain, while the non-initiator may seem like an overly emotional victim.

I believe that this difference between the initiator and non-initiator is what often triggers and fuels the combative behavior exhibited in many divorce proceedings.

Jeremy: Since neither person can change when they began processing the reality of divorce, are there ways they can at least avoid some of the common pitfalls?

Marc: Yes, I believe the answer can be found in being compassionate and respectful of your soon-to-be-ex-spouse rather than using the divorce process to punish and penalize them. Despite how you may currently feel about them, you and your children will be much better off if you focus on the big picture, rather than resorting to pettiness. For one reason or another, many people feel the need to "inflict" the divorce onto their spouse. They declare, "I've met with lawyers, and I have filed papers! Deal with it!"

As you can imagine, this type of announcement rarely elicits a positive outcome.

If you are the initiator of the divorce, I recommend you ask yourself questions such as:

- "How can I create the best possible outcome for my family?"

- "How can we avoid a costly, protracted litigation?"

- "How can I constructively influence the result of this transition?"

Instead of unilaterally proclaiming an end to the relationship, consider inviting your spouse to a frank conversation about the state of your relationship and the options that you both are facing. Your spouse doesn't have to agree with you, but at least you made the effort to include them in the decision.

Remember, how you approach your divorce is far more impactful than the divorce itself. Your goal should be to restructure the household; not to destroy your family.

Jeremy: You once said that "divorce is a narcissistic struggle where children are often the collateral damage."

Marc: Yes, combative parents often forget about their children. The divorce becomes acrimonious, where each parent focuses more on punishing the other than trying to do what's best for their children. Too often parents ignore or are oblivious to their children's emotions and needs. Rather than doing what is in their children's best interest, they treat their children like possessions.

Jeremy: When parents behave selfishly and ignore their children's needs, how do you coach them?

Marc: I remind them that we don't own our children. We're more like stewards guiding and nurturing them into adulthood. It's vital that we consider what's best for the children, even when it conflicts with one's immediate goals and desires. In divorce, what one wants in the short-term is rarely in alignment with what they want over the long-term.

More often than not, parents look back at how they chose to proceed through their divorce with many regrets. There are many things they would have done differently. As a coach, I try to help my clients think beyond the next five minutes or even five months. I help them consider the long-term consequences of how they approach their divorce.

People have been getting divorced for a long time, yet we continue to make the same mistakes. I always ask my clients, "Why not learn from the mistakes of others?"

Jeremy: In previous conversations, you shared your coaching process known as "The 5 Steps to a Mindful Divorce." Can you identify what they are, and in a sentence or two, describe each?

The Five Steps to a Mindful Divorce

Marc: The Five Steps to a Mindful Divorce are:

Step 1: Acceptance

Accept what is. You're getting a divorce. There's a lot of emotional baggage that comes with divorce. Don't let it cloud your judgment; you have a lot of work to do. Others may be counting on you. It's time to get focused and clear.

Step 2: Accountability

You married this person. Now one or both of you want a divorce. Take responsibility for your actions, and more importantly, assume the responsibility for protecting and nurturing your children through this stressful and emotional time. Your kids didn't ask for this divorce; they shouldn't have to suffer too. So don't forget about your children's needs.

Step 3: Compassion.

Forgive yourself. Don't beat yourself up. There are two sides to every story. We all make mistakes. You're not the first. None of us is perfect. Focus on being your best self and making the most of these new circumstances.

Step 4: Choice

This step will define your character for many years to come. Regardless of your spouse's actions or inactions, are you going to make this divorce easy or difficult? I'm not encouraging you to give up. I'm encouraging you to think into the future and powerfully choose how you want to look back at this time in your life; how you want your children, your family, and friends to reflect back on it too. If there is ever a moment to take the high road, this may be it.

Step 5: Creation

Creation is the inspiring step! It's where you get to look into the future with hope and excitement. Yes, you may feel scared and vulnerable, too. But that's natural. You're not alone. We survived and so will you. Do some soul-searching and figure out how to turn these lemons into lemonade.

While it may seem paradoxical, I believe that with time and perspective divorce can be a powerful, positive transformational process where one can develop greater self-awareness, self-expression, and fulfillment than ever before. But it will take time, introspection and healing.

Jeremy: Well said. And, finally, how can the reader learn more about you and your coaching process?

Marc: They can reach out to me through my website at Quantum Resolution Coaching, as well as schedule a complimentary discovery session to see if working with a coach makes sense for them.

Key Takeaways

√   **Tame your highly competitive nature.**

√   **Consider what it really means to "win" in family court.**

√   **Focus on restructuring your family, not destroying it.**

√   **Recognize your role as the "initiator" or the "non-initiator."**

√   **Apply these Five Steps for a Mindful Divorce:**

        1. **Acceptance**

        2. **Accountability**

        3. **Compassion**

        4. **Choice**

        5. **Creation**

ABOUT MARC LEVEY, CDC®

Marc Levey is a CDC Certified Divorce Coach®, Conflict Resolution Specialist and divorced father of three. As the founder of Quantum Resolution Coaching, Marc specializes in coaching highly competitive professionals including athletes, entertainers and executives through milestone transitions including high conflict divorce.

Marc feels fortunate that over his 25-year career as an award-winning artist, author, inspirational speaker, and coach, he has had the opportunity to not only work with hundreds of extraordinary everyday people, but also with some of the most influential figures in entertainment, sports and technology.

Greatly influenced by his experience living and studying in Japan, Marc marries Eastern principles with the practical realities of Western life into his coaching and writing including his book, "The Art of Mindful Divorce." Integrating a distinctly zen-inspired approach into his coaching practice, Marc helps clients resolve conflict and create balance in their professional and personal lives through transformational growth and development.

BUSINESS: Quantum Resolution Coaching

WEBSITE: www.quantum-resolution.com

EMAIL: m@quantum-resolution.com

PHONE: 310.853.3065

LOCATION: Beverly Hills, CA

CHAPTER FOUR

EFFECTIVE COMMUNICATION

Interview with **Glenys Reeves**, CDC®, MA, CEC, PCC

> *"The difference between the right word and the almost right word is the difference between lightning and the lightning bug."* — *Mark Twain*

Jeremy: Glenys, can you share a little bit about the topic you will be discussing with us?

Glenys: My topic is effective communication practices when you're going through a separation or divorce, and the importance of communicating effectively with your former partner for your own mental health and being able to move forward.

Jeremy: Please expound more on your personal background, and what inspired you to become a divorce coach.

Glenys: Sure, I'm happy to do that Jeremy. I was involved in family law mediation for close to fifteen years. I specifically did a lot of work with divorcing couples helping them with their parenting plans. During this time, it became apparent to me that people going through separation and divorce needed to express their needs and listen to the other party. If they were able to do this, they were much more effective at being able to work through their issues and to make this life transition easier.

There is always a lot of emotions when experiencing a separation or divorce, and knowing how to work through this and communicate assertively without getting caught up in emotions is essential. I always used to think about this and would wonder what it would be like for me. It wasn't until I experienced my divorce did I realize how difficult it was. Even though I knew all the skills necessary to maneuver through it, I still struggled to communicate in a way that was effective for me. I must admit that I didn't always use the best skill, and I guess that brought home to me how important this was.

It was at this point that I looked at the whole area of divorce coaching, and went and did my training because I think it's critical that we display our best self. With my coaching background, I knew what an empowering process it could be, so I wanted to expand my practice so I could do transition coaching as well. That's how I ended up as a divorce coach.

Jeremy: So often we learn from our experiences, and it inspires us to share what we learned with other people as well.

Glenys, why is communication so important during divorce? Obviously, communication is necessary for all aspects of our life, but it is of particular importance when experiencing conflict. Can you share more on this importance?

Glenys: When a relationship breaks down, there are numerous decisions to be made. These can be financial decisions, decisions around property, and often there are children involved, so there need to be decisions made in regards to parenting plans. Typically, communication hasn't been great in a relationship, and that may have led to the actual relationship breakdown. There is a need to explore how to communicate during a relationship transition because it is often full of a variety of emotions. If individuals going through separation or divorce are not able to express their point of view rationally in negotiations, they often go away feeling frustrated. Some have long-term regrets because their decisions are going to affect their future.

Also, when needing to develop co-parenting plans, it's important that there is good communication established from the beginning, as this often sets the tone for long-term communication. Even though you've made the decision not to be a couple anymore, the fact is that you still have to be parents together, and you need to figure out how to do that. That's why it's paramount that there is effective communication through this whole process.

Jeremy: When it comes to actually communicating with one's ex, what common mistakes do people make?

Glenys: I think the biggest mistake is we often let emotions override our ability to think logically about what is best for us, and that immediate reaction is not going to get us the long-term effects that we need. People often become outraged and frustrated, and this can get in the way of reason. We know that when we get angry, physically our body goes into what's called fight or flight. When this happens our ability to reason and express ourselves effectively is significantly decreased. Think about it, have you ever been angry and said things you regret, that when you calm down, wish you hadn't said them? That's because our body has gone into that fight or flight response and we do not think clearly.

The other problem, as I mentioned before, is many relationships break down because of poor communication. It's not realistic to think when you're going through this emotional time, that these previous patterns are going to change unless we consciously take the time to think about this, and strategize on how we need to do things differently. I think that's why coaching is so effective because everyone does have the capacity to reflect on how they can communicate differently. I think a coach can help individuals explore this, and develop actions so they can take this to move forward and communicate differently through this process.

Jeremy: That's great advice regarding fight or flight mode, and how it makes it difficult to behave rationally when we're in that state. I can see how having the guidance of coaching helps us cultivate self-awareness and a better understanding when we're acting in an irrational way versus when we're in our sound mind.

Glenys: Absolutely, because a coach's role is to become a partner, both a thinking partner and a learning partner. By asking our clients compelling questions, it can change people's perspective and get them to take a look at how they can do things differently.

Jeremy: Can you go into more detail of how a parent can communicate more effectively with their ex? Are there specific questions or techniques that they can learn, and apply to their current situation?

Glenys: Of course there are, and I've done a lot of work around effective communications especially in conflict. I think what we have to remember is we call it communication 'skills' for a reason. It's because they're skill-based. When I do programs around that, I often talk about most of us are born with the ability to speak. None of us is necessarily born with the capacity to be an effective communicator because that requires skills, just like the skills we learn for a job or for a sport. We need to understand what they are; we need to practice them, and they need to become part of who we are. A critical part of communication is listening. Most of us are born with the ability to hear, but very few of us are born to be active or supportive listeners. If we want to learn those new skills, we absolutely can.

The first thing we need to do is take a look at what our unhealthy patterns of communication are. We need to be honest with ourselves in regards to how this is affecting our ability to move forward. When we get caught up in anger and frustration, we can't move forward. Separation and divorce are a transition. We want to transition out of that and transition into the new way of doing things.

Once we're able to identify what's not working for us, then we need to talk about what might work better. That's where we can start to discover new skills and learn ways to practice them, so they become part of who we are as a communicator. I always tell people when they're learning new communication skills, and encounter conflict, don't think that these new skills will come automatically or easily right away, you need to practice them. You have to think of people and situations that are safe where you can practice the new skills you are learning. You can even practice effective communication beyond conflictual situations. A lot of these skills can be implemented and practiced in positive conversations. Eventually, it just becomes who we are.

A communication skill I've found useful for people experiencing separation or divorce is assertive communication, or asking for what you want in a respectful way. It includes describing a behavior in a very objective measurable way; including how you feel and by using "I language" because you own that feeling. It includes talking about what could be done differently and what the change or effect will be if people can do it that way.

Then there is supportive listening. Often as I said before when people think about listening, they think about hearing, but there are different stages of the listening process. One of the stages is to understand. You have to understand where that other person is coming from. We do that by asking open questions and then clarifying back your understanding through paraphrasing. We listen to understand the other point of view. Paraphrasing isn't just about repeating back what you hear, but it's also repeating back what you see because often people are giving us a message verbally, but non-verbally they're giving us another message. If you want to be a supportive listener, you want to ensure that you're understanding all of those messages.

The other thing is that you have to keep an open framework through this. I often like to use the mantra you need to 'stay curious, not judgmental.' Often the person we spent all that time with, our former partner, is the one who knows how to trigger us the easiest. Keep an open mindset, try to understand, and try not to judge what they say is so important if you are going to be successful in your conversations.

Once we're able to do that, we can start to reframe it. Start to take a look at opportunities that the situation may present. I remember that happening to me with a friend when I was down and not understanding where I was going to go. The question that was asked to me is, "What opportunities might this have? Are you excited about this?" It was a great way to reframe what my new transition was going to look like. Once you're able to look at these opportunities that the situation may present, then you can start to acknowledge that both of you are having feelings around this, and indicate that you're starting to try and understand those feelings.

When we're in conflictual situations, we have to get out of our positions, and we need to get down to our interests, because if I'm positional, what I'm doing is saying this is a solution to the problem. Because we're in conflict, the other person has a different position or a different solution. If I start to understand what's important about that solution to the other person, then I'm moving to being interest-based and then I can negotiate on what's important to you, and what's important to me versus offering ultimatums through the conversation.

Jeremy: Those are great points. The concept of being interest-based aligns well with collaborative law or mediation, whereas in family court, you have more of an adversarial process, and it is always position-based.

Can you think of an example of a role play to help define these concepts?

Glenys: Yes, I can certainly think of an example. You have two parents, and they're talking about a parenting plan, and arguing about the time that needs to be spent at each parent's home. One parent explains that the reason the kids cannot go to the other parent's during the week is because that parent does not adhere to a specific bedtime. The other parent is saying, "You can't tell me what to do when the kids are at my house as I do things my way, and I think my bedtime is quite appropriate." If they try to negotiate; one parent saying their way is appropriate, the other saying it is not appropriate, they're never going to get anywhere.

If you can ask the question, "What's important to you about being able to make those decisions when the children are at your house?" The one parent may say, "I want to feel that when they are at my house, I'm the one that's the parent, and I'm able to have some control over that relationship, and on what the routine in the house looks like." Then you may sit with the other parent, who is talking about their concerns about bedtime, and they may say, "You know what's important to me? Consistency. If I make them go to bed at 8:00 pm and they go to the other parent's house, and they don't go to bed until 10:00 pm, there is inconsistency, and I need consistency."

If we explore this from an interest-base perspective, then we are discussing what consistency between the homes needs to look like and also how decisions are made for the children when they are in each parent's home. That is a totally different conversation than arguing about the time the kids need to go to bed.

Jeremy: How would you say non-defensive yet assertive communication techniques benefit not just the parents but the children as well?

Glenys: The problem is, like it or not, kids always get caught in the cross-fire. If parents can communicate in an effective way through assertive communication and listen and understand each other, the kids see that. They see that mom and dad are working together to try to establish a routine that's going to work.

Let's face facts, separation and divorce is a real transition for kids as well. They've been living in one home, now they're going to be living in two homes, sometimes it means maybe they're living in the same home, but mom and dad are coming back and forth. I just think as parents; anytime we can demonstrate communication skills that are more effective through assertive language and supportive listening and we start to use that in all parts of our lives, kids start to model this as well.

Jeremy: Can you share an example of a client that you worked with that wasn't communicating effectively with their ex and through their walk with you were able to learn and apply these skills?

Glenys: Through my divorce coaching practice, I've had numerous clients who are in a variety of situations. What they found is that by exploring communication patterns and making a plan on how to do things differently, has been very effective for them to move forward. Some of these have been clients who are dealing with issues in their professional life and others in their personal life.

A common example is when they try to communicate with their former partner and are unable to solve any issues as they "trigger" each other when they try to talk. By coaching them and asking them to think of situations where they have seen conflict solved effectively, clients can identify how they need to do things differently. By recognizing the communication techniques they are not using and identify ones that might be more effective, they can formulate a plan on how they plan on practicing and using these skills. One of my clients had been arguing over property for months. By coaching on communication techniques, she was able to identify some new strategies, understand her anger triggers better and went back into negotiation and was able to come to an agreement.

As I said before, the biggest challenge I see with individuals going through separation and divorce, is they tend to be easily triggered by the other person. When they do get triggered, they revert to old patterns. Sometimes the coaching is around just exploring what triggers them and help them become more self-aware about how this happens. If they can stop it at that point, they're much more likely to be effective as they move forward.

For example, I get them thinking about what occurs when they have a conversation with their former partner and evaluate how successful it was. Then contrast that with times when they felt positive about outcomes of a conversation. This doesn't necessarily always have to be a conversation with their former partner; it can be a conversation with someone else in which they felt the conversation went well. Then they can evaluate what skills were effective, and see how they can bring those across to conversations they are having with their ex. If they can't remember any conversations they felt positive about, then I have them brainstorm in regards to individuals who they see as really effective communicators. Then talk about what they observe in those conversations and how they can bring this into their own communication patterns.

The exploration of what's positional and what's being interest-based is always a great thing to coach and to help them look forward. Often I'll ask a question such as, "Five years from now, when you look back on this time in your life, what do you want to remember?" I think all of us will say we want to remember being our best selves. Then we can talk about "What does that need to look like now so this can be your memory?" It has to be action-based coaching. You can have an excellent supportive conversation with someone, but at the end of the coaching conversation, they should have strategic actions that they understand. Things that they can do that are going to move them forward in their ability to communicate more effectively. I always ask questions on a scale of 1 to 10; 1 equals not being committed, to 10 which is being totally committed to taking action. If it's anything less than a 10, we talk about what needs to change to get them to a 10.

Then they need to decide what they're going to do to hold themselves accountable. Maybe we talk about what they're going to practice. I had one situation where a client was frightened she was going to be triggered, so we strategized around how she was going to work around this with her lawyer. Her lawyer would pick up if she was being triggered and then give her some non-verbal sign, so she realized that's what was happening, so she could start to focus more on her communication and move forward. We talked about what was important to her about effective communication and how this could change the outcome of the negotiations with her former partner. Your job as a coach is to get people thinking differently.

I've had numerous people come back to me who've been much happier and successful in their interactions. Often people are feeling totally disempowered. I had a client who felt really "beat up" after she had been through a mediation session. Through coaching about effective communication and allowing her an opportunity to practice and think about it, she came back to the next coaching session and felt much more empowered compared to being overpowered. That was a positive situation for her; she was able to negotiate much more effectively in her mediation sessions. Once again it reinforced to me how important communication skills are.

Jeremy: I like what you said regarding taking the long view. Think about having a conversation with your kids ten or fifteen years from now and you're advising them on their relationships and things that you may have done differently. If we put ourselves in the future now, we can elicit those behavioral changes in the present rather than live with regrets later.

Glenys, do have any suggestions on how someone can stay calm and focused when in a stressful divorce situation?

Glenys: Yes, I have seven self-coaching questions one can ask themselves in these type of situations.

Self-Coaching Questions and Rationale

Question 1: What is my interest in this solution?

Remember if you are giving a solution that is a position

Question 2: What is important about this solution to me?

This will help you define your interest

Questions 3 and 4: What emotion am I feeling? What is the most non-confrontational way to explain this?

Make sure you express how you are feeling. As human beings, we relate on a feeling level.

REMEMBER assertive "I language" helps explain your point of view and helps prevent defensiveness in others as you "own" your feelings.

Question 5: What might be the interest of the other person?

Stay curious, ask questions and clarify your understanding. (Start your questions with Who, What, How, When, and you will gather more information)

By "seeking to understand" the other person's point of view it prevents you from becoming judgmental (Mantra: "curious not judgmental")

Question 6: What triggers me?

Understand your anger triggers and your personal "warning" signs that you are getting upset.

Then have your positive mantra to keep you focused. (i.e. "I can do this.")

Question 7: What do I want to remember about who I was during this transition?

Focus on the future and how you want to be remembered. This helps you to remain your "best self."

By keeping this as your focus, you have a better chance of negotiating a positive solution for everyone involved.

Jeremy: In closing, is there one last thing that you feel the reader should remember?

Glenys: Communication requires skills, and we all have the ability to learn those skills, we all have the ability to make those changes. I just want people to understand never give up; there are always different ways to do things.

Jeremy: Perfect, thank you Glenys. If somebody wants to get a hold of you, what's the best way for them to reach out to you?

Glenys: The best way for them to reach out to me would be through text. My text number is 780.808.5779.

Key Takeaways

Communication Tips on Negotiating a Positive Divorce Solution:

√   **Understand your interest in the solution.**

√   **Define what is important to you.**

√   **Express how you are feeling – use "I Language."**

√   **Ask questions using "Who, What, How, When" to clarify your understanding.**

√   **Understand your anger triggers and implement your positive mantra to maintain focus.**

√   **Focus on the future and how you want to be remembered during your divorce.**

ABOUT GLENYS REEVES, CDC®, MA, CEC, PCC

Glenys has worked in the divorce field as a mediator and as a coach. She holds certifications as an Executive Coach and CDC Certified Divorce Coach®. She has also received her Professional Coach Certification through the International Coach Federation.

Glenys has a special interest in personal leadership. This developed while she was completing her MA in leadership and she believes that people need to personally lead as they navigate through separation and divorce.

During the time Glenys practiced mediation she recognized the need for individuals to remain their "best-self" to be able to take the high road while transitioning to their new life.

Personally, she has had to navigate through her own life transition and recognized that no matter what experience or training you have, a coach who assists you to remain your "best-self" is invaluable.

When not working, Glenys and her partner enjoy travelling, often abroad to spend time with her two adult children.

BUSINESS: Reeves Coaching and Consulting

WEBSITE: www.exertandexcelcoaching.com

EMAIL: gmreevesgibbs@gmail.com

PHONE: 780.808.5779

LOCATION: Lloydminster, AB, Canada

CHAPTER FIVE

DETOXING THE TRAUMA OF DIVORCE

Interview with **Lori A. Burton-Cluxton**, MSW, CDC®

> *"Trust your gut! Your head will rationalize, your heart is emotionally involved...always trust your gut...it's God's whisper. It's instinct."* — *Lori Burton-Cluxton*

Jeremy: Lori, tell me a little bit about your practice, Advantage Point Coaching, and what types of people you help.

Lori: Advantage Point Coaching is a "come-as-you-are" location for women to find support, guidance, resources, and solutions. I serve women who are in one of the three phases of divorce: pre-divorce, during the process of divorce, or post-divorce. I also help those who are experiencing behaviors or symptomologies of trauma or crisis related to their divorce that is interfering with their dailiness of life.

I am a Certified Divorce Coach and a certified trauma recovery coach. I specialize in working with women, so that they have security, confidence, and hope, knowing they have a happy, well-adjusted life and family.

Jeremy: So you help women in all phases of divorce; whether it's pre-divorce, during a divorce, or post-divorce?

Lori: Correct. Women and their families are a passion of mine. A goal for me is that by working with them, they would feel heard and understood, walking away feeling better than when they came, and ultimately, living their lives authentically. That's huge, being able to live their lives authentically and with fewer regrets.

Jeremy: Many people get into this field because of life experiences that inspired them to help people. Can you share with us what inspired you to become a Certified Divorce Coach and help people?

Lori: It was in high school. When I was in tenth grade, I was asked to be a peer tutor. I found out then that if I asked people the right questions, they could find within themselves the right answers. My friends would often turn to me for advice, and say, "Hey, Lori, can I talk to you about this?" Or, "Please don't tell anyone about this, but what do you think?" Then we would just brainstorm, and I found myself taking a passion to it; naturally and instinctively it became my lifestyle and my career.

I found myself drawn to it. Often, I say my career chose me. Social justice concerns of the world or my community; advocating for people, missions, and philanthropy. These are themes that have become a central part of what defines me.

Jeremy: In your work, are there any particular common challenges, obstacles, or misconceptions that you find people have that may prevent

them from achieving the outcome that you want to help them with or that they're seeking?

Lori: Jeremy, that's a great question. And, it's one people often ask me. Breaking it down to the lowest common denominator, I believe it is that often people don't believe in themselves. They don't have faith in themselves. They may believe more in what other people have to say about them, or what other people think — that is a common pit-fall.

Divorce can be a major life crisis, and when a person goes through it, they can feel like they've been hit by a train wreck in all areas of life: work, finances, health, family, friends, romance, and personal growth. It's, also, a grieving process. Everyone's emotions are running high. People say a lot of different things. Many of the things people say are negative. And, this can be exhausting.

There are many positive steps people can take to turn things around and start believing in themselves. For example, they may detox their life from the negative stuff - the aggressive, intimidating, dominating, manipulative people or things in their life. Many people may say to you that maybe you're just depressed. Well, going through a divorce or a major life crisis isn't exactly delightful, but it doesn't necessarily mean you need a diagnosis of "depressive disorder" either. You are feeling sad, and will be for a temporary time. Sadness and grieving are normal emotions. Allow yourself to go through it in a reasonable amount of time. If in doubt, check with your doctor. Also, check your environment before you diagnose yourself with depression or low self-esteem. Make sure you are not, in fact, surrounded by unhealthy people.

Often, you just have to observe your environment and start detoxing it. Remove yourself from the negativity that is in your life, and ask yourself, "What am I inviting in?" Remind yourself that you are what you eat, drink, listen to, watch and read. Make sure you surround yourself with healthy, positive, encouraging, uplifting and supportive people. Surround yourself with people who add value and energy to your life, and people who like you and believe in you.

Jeremy: You mentioned a process — ways to deal with trauma. Can you talk about what that process is?

Lori: With some women, once we've been chatting for a bit, and we've been walking down the path together of their personal story, we may come to a point. Based on some of the things I've heard, I may ask, "May I interrupt and share a few tools that may help you see yourself in a different perspective?" I begin by sharing that they are "normal." By doing so, they can normalize the behaviors and symptomologies that they may have been sharing with me.

Now, let me go into further detail on the process...

Step One: Recognize Common Reactions to Trauma

- Shock, denial or disbelief that it happened.

- Ashamed, embarrassed or guilty feelings.

- Angry, irritable or short-tempered.

- Sadness, crying spells or depression.

- Thinking about suicide or wanting to get away from everything.

- Feeling a loss of control in their life, or with their options.

- Less interest in friends; not wanting to socialize as much.

- Loss of trust in others or in their decision-making.

- Difficulty with concentration; forgetting everyday things.

- Changes in sleeping patterns (insomnia or over-sleeping).

- Nightmares or flashbacks about what happened.

- Changes in appetite and food intake (more or less).

- Feeling insecure or uncertain about the future.

- Fears about being alone or about the future.

- Feeling on guard, jumpy or easily startled.

- Isolating, staying alone more often (less time with family or friends).

- Feeling more anxious, nervous or scared.

- Feeling numb or having a hard time expressing their emotions.

Anyone going through divorce experiences a whole range of emotions. They're going through a traumatic time, a major life crisis, so first we discuss common reactions to trauma. I have them read these out loud, because when I stop them in their story, they're talking about some symptomologies and behaviors that make them feel like they're going crazy. Or, they've shared with me that somebody's told them that they're going crazy, they must be depressed, or any number of other things.

I have them read out loud a list of some common characteristics to trauma. After they start reading from the list, they begin to see that they are experiencing "normal" responses to an "abnormal" event. This is an important point: they are experiencing "normal" responses to an "abnormal" event. You can see them begin to relax and think, "Wow. That just makes so much sense." And, for a moment, they can realize that, yes, this too will pass; I'm not going crazy. So we just reinforce that their mind, body, and spirit is in a current state of high stress, and with healthy coping mechanisms, they will get through this.

Step Two: Recognize Common Reactions by Friends, Family & Relatives

Your friends, family or relatives may react in one or more of the following ways:

- Feel revengeful and want to hurt the offender.

- Feel uncomfortable about what to say or whether to talk about it.

- Ask several questions and want to know every-thing that happened.

- Remain neutral and try not to take sides if they know both the loved one and the offender.

- Blame the loved one for things they may have done to put themselves at risk.

- Blame themselves for not doing something to prevent it.

- Want to care for and protect the loved one.

- Want to control the situation and make decisions about what to do.

- Disagree with the decisions the loved one made.

- Express anger or frustration that it happened or at the court process.

- Feel sad and hurt that this happened.

- Tell other people about what happened without asking first.

- Want the person to be "over it" sooner than they are ready.

- Feel closer to their loved one for sharing this difficult time.

- Not know what to say, so they don't say anything.

- Be available to their loved one, any time of day or night.

None of these are unusual; they all are all typical reactions. But sometimes people become uncomfortable; they are unsure what to say, or they don't know if they should talk about their situation in front of them. After reviewing these, and even role-playing their responses, they will feel more comfortable that they don't need to become overly concerned. They can then recognize that these reactions are in no way a personal attack on them: "I am not being singled out. It isn't just me." When they start to see themselves again on that page from friends and family, it makes them feel much better.

Step Three: Create a Non-Specific Ten-Second Commercial

I encourage clients to create an authentic, nonspecific ten-second "commercial" they can use as a response. The reason for this is so that the person going through the divorce doesn't get caught off guard by people coming up to them at the grocery store, at the gym, or at school when they're with their kids. People may come up to them to ask them questions about the divorce, or the event, or whatever it is that they're going through in this crisis. Many people become avoidant because of this. They may isolate or avoid places they previously frequented because they don't want to answer questions. By having a ten-second commercial, a one-sentence explanation, they will feel better prepared and more comfortable.

For example:

> "Billy and I are no longer married. I appreciate your concern, the kids and I would welcome your prayers."

> "Yeah, but I heard…"

> "Billy and I are no longer married. I appreciate your concern, the kids and I would welcome your prayers."

Sometimes people can be rude and intrusive at times, but there's no need to hide from them, and when you're pre-pared to answer their questions — you repeat that commercial every time -- you feel safe, secure, and empowered. And by the third time of repeating that commercial to the same person, they've concluded you aren't going to tell them because it's none of their business, it's not their concern, and you can go on about your business and your day. It's very empowering. They feel like, "Wow, that is exactly what I needed."

Along with the third step, I encourage or just ask how would you feel about sharing that little commercial with your inside circle, with those that you trust. Because your kids, they also need to know what to say; they're not equipped to know how to answer all of the questions sometimes, and it's very comforting for them to know how to respond when they encounter similar situations.

The same applies to parents and grandparents, brothers and sisters, or whoever your inner circle may include. You bring them around; write it on a three-by-five card and say, "Here it is. This is our commercial, our unified front. And this is what you can say." It can be a great tool.

Case Study: "Maggie"

An excellent case example of trauma recovery is "Maggie". Maggie was a married mother of four children, upper middle class, going through a divorce and child custody case, with a history of domestic violence. Due to her estranged husband's career, there was no documentation of the domestic violence up to this point and due to the coercive controlling behavior of a batterer and their "charm", nobody believed this was happening behind closed doors. After seeking coaching which led her to other legal resource assistance, Maggie found the support and guidance she was looking for. A turning point was when she was immediately awarded a protection order. She was believed.

In following the three step process, in **Step One: Recognize Common Reactions to Trauma**; Maggie was able to see that she was having normal reactions to an abnormal event and that she was not what her estranged husband was telling her she was. She also realized, her children were having traumatic reactions too, appropriate to their age. Maggie made the conscious decision to be the example her children needed her to be.

In **Step Two: Recognize Common Reactions by Friends and Family**; Maggie faced her emotions through coaching and pulled together a strong support team. A part of her group coaching was a self-defense class. This was very empowering for her and helped her find her voice and the warrior within.

In **Step Three: Create a Non-Specific Ten-Second Commercial**: Maggie and her children thrived with confidence and swiftly moved themselves from victim mentality into one of strength and perseverance. After a fourteen-month process, Maggie was given custody of all four of her children, and has become a coach herself!

Jeremy: I think the "Non-Specific Ten-Second Commercial" is excellent advice, not just for the person going through the divorce, but for others who are impacted to be able to have that sentence. You don't have to go into negativity, blame, or anything like that. It prevents us from going into negative triggers or negative emotions.

Do you have any suggestions, any advice, such as "do's and don'ts," or other tips that people might find helpful?

Lori: Yes, let's start with some "Divorce Don'ts."

Divorce Don'ts...

Don't be afraid to call the police in situations where there is domestic violence.

Since I deal with trauma and different things like domestic violence, there are some instances in my line of work, where there are Civil Protection Orders (CPO's) involved. It's not your "cut and dry" divorce. Safety is a higher risk. Sometimes there are stalking orders or other things like that. In these situations, police reports can be crucial in supporting your case.

They're clearly not necessary for all cases, nor am I talking about the occasional dropping off the kids ten minutes late or something like that. But in some situations, especially when there is a history of domestic violence, to avoid "he said, she said" debates, police reports can be especially important to establish a paper trail for court documentation. By doing so, you also send the message that you're going to be proactive, resourceful, and not going to tolerate being harassed. You're standing up for yourself and your family.

Don't engage in the negative when you are baited.

Sometimes an ex-spouse will harass you by sending what I call, a nasty gram, through email, text, or on the phone. I encourage you not to take the bait; don't argue with your spouse, with the father or mother of your children. Don't do this in person or in front of the kids. It's just not worth it. Your focus should be on the children and the future. I advise people that if you cannot exercise discipline by re-fusing to engage in the negative, you could lose custody of your kids. I cannot enforce that enough.

Don't badmouth your ex.

Don't badmouth your ex in front of your children, your family or others.

Taking the high road is better for your child, and it won't come back to bite you later. Don't ever forget that your kids are half of your ex-spouse, and they see themselves as half of their father or mother. If you engage in bad-mouthing the other parent, they may feel ashamed of themselves because they hear all the negativity, and in their minds, internalize it, believing what they hear, and that they are half of that, so they must be that too.

You know the psychological warfare that this plays on them. Allow your child to form their own opinions, and try to answer their questions about the situation as respect-fully and as age-appropriately as possible. Hate has no place in the family home. It just doesn't.

Divorce Do's...

Do utilize your community resources.

There are some excellent community resources and organizations available to help and assist you with free services. Overcome the fear or the pride of asking for help. We all need it from time to time. Your turn to help others will come, and you can assist them and pay that forward.

Do have regular coaching sessions.

Coaching can help you keep your eye on your goals, and to assist you in reaching your desired outcomes.

Do maintain a resource list of professionals who are competent in their fields.

The community resources I mentioned can help you with this; so can your coach. There are other professionals you may need who are competent in their field.

Do live with integrity.

Live with integrity and do not distort the truth or behave in a manner that your ex can use against you in court.

Do remember that attitude is everything.

Life is ten percent what happens to you, and ninety percent on how you respond to it. So choose optimism and to live in a positive manner, not only for yourself but for your children.

Do understand that you can only control what goes on in your own home.

You have only so much time to spend with your children, so provide loving limits and structure. You cannot control what goes on when they are on a visitation with their father or their mother. You can only control what happens in your home. Your relationship with your child is your relationship with your child, and the relationship they have with your ex — their father or mother — is their relationship. Therefore, you should not try to intervene. If you attempt to interfere with this relationship, they'll come to resent you for it later. Safety first and adhere to the divorce decree.

Jeremy: Those are great tips. Now, if there's one lesson, one critical thing that you think everybody should consider or be cognizant of, what would that be?

Lori: Acknowledge, recognize and believe you are the expert in your life, and that you always have choices.

For instance, when something happens, think for a moment and ask yourself:

- What are my choices here?

- What are my options?

- What resources do I have available?

- What do I need to do?

- What's missing?

- What's going to get me to where I want to go?

- Is this acceptable?

- Can I change it? (Some things we can't change.)

- Who will walk with me through this?

Again, surround yourself with positivity. Find somebody who's going to be positive, supportive, and uplifting — who can walk with you through this temporary situation.

Once you realize that you aren't backed into a corner on an issue or a decision, there are choices, and that there are options for those choices. That there are experts to assist you in the decision-making. Recognizing it's not all just you, you're not alone. It can be so liberating, and you'll feel confident that you can make it through to the other side. Especially when you know and understand your triggers through all of those things, because there are some very common triggers people encounter as they are going through difficult circumstances.

Common Triggers

- Sounds

- Smells

- Colors

- Movements

- Objects

- Anniversaries

- Holidays

- Any event or situation that resembles/symbolizes the trauma

But just knowing that you are the expert in your life and that you always have choices, that you can and will overcome — can be one of the best things to help you through life's peaks and valleys.

Jeremy: I like that a lot, because life is about choices, and as you said, "Life is ten percent about what happens to you and ninety percent about how we react to it."

Key Takeaways

√   **BElieve in YOUrself.**

√   **Detox from the negative in your life immediately.**

√   **You are having normal responses to an abnormal event.**

√   **Always Trust Your Gut!**

√   **Attitude is Everything!! 90% of life is influenced by your attitude. Choose to lift a person's day!**

To find out more about Lori and her services, call or text 513.445.4842, or my website: www.advantagepointcoaching.com. She is also available via Skype (lori.bc1). You can "like" Lori's Facebook page at: www.facebook.com/AdvantagePointCoachingLLC. Lori is passionate about connecting with people going through life's transitions.

ABOUT LORI A. BURTON-CLUXTON, MSW, CDC®

Lori Burton-Cluxton is CEO of Advantage Point Coaching, LLC, a present-future focused, strengths and faith-based organization. She is a CDC Certified Divorce Coach® and Certified Trauma Recovery Coach, an M.S.W., with all other degrees, licensures, and certifications in her 35 years of experience being in sociology, psychology, teaching, and coaching.

Lori's diverse background dealing with divorce, child welfare, counseling, domestic violence, sexual assault, substance abuse, teaching, and investigations has exposed her to many challenges that women and their families face. She believes that women are the expert in their lives, and co-partners with them to accomplish what they want to achieve; encouraging self-discovery and client-generated solutions and strategies.

With the use of listening and skillfulness, Lori is a master at connecting with others to make those she works with feel confident and secure that they will be heard and understood in working through their concern with clarity and resolve. Her passion is assisting couples back on the path to reconciliation when that is their choice; supporting the blended family, and helping those going through divorce co-parent and create a healthy future for their children.

BUSINESS: Advantage Point Coaching, LLC

WEBSITE: www.advantagepointcoaching.com

SKYPE: lori.bc1

EMAIL: lori@advantagepointcoaching.com

PHONE: 513.445.4842

LOCATION: Mason, OH

FACEBOOK: www.facebook.com/AdvantagePointCoachingLLC

LINKEDIN: www.linkedin.com/in/lori-burton-cluxton-447b0995

TWITTER: @LoriAdvanPoint

PART 2:

CHANGING THE PROCESS FOR

DECISION-MAKING

"The most difficult thing is the decision to act, the rest is merely tenacity. The fears are paper tigers. You can do anything you decide to do. You can act to change and control your life; and the procedure, the process is its own reward." ~Amelia Earhart

CHAPTER SIX

THE COMEBACK ROADMAP

Interview with **Pamela Y. Dykes**, Ph.D., CDC®,

ACC, MCM, Florida Supreme Court Certified Family

Mediator

"If you want to make a COMEBACK you must take the high road, and to take the high road you must consider everyone involved! It's not about winning the war, it's about winning the battle for yourself and your children."
— *Pamela Dykes*

"Use your set back as a set up for your comeback." —
Tim Storey and Joel Osteen

Jeremy: Pamela, can you share a little bit about your divorce coaching practice and what inspired you to become a divorce coach?

Pamela: Before I became a divorce coach, I was writing a book called "Diary of a Comeback Mom" because I was desperate to get back into the workforce. I started interviewing women who had an interesting comeback story. I interviewed three women, one had become a ship captain, one had lost one hundred pounds on her own, and the other had overcome domestic violence, and they're all thriving in life now.

When I interviewed them, I wanted to know their story about their comeback and how they were able to move into or onto something new. However, when I contacted them, all of their responses were, "Oh sure, I'll tell you my story, but I'm going through a horrible divorce. Does that impact you wanting to interview me?" Of course not. That was perfect, and their stories were inspiring.

Around six months later, my husband told me that he no longer wanted to be married, and within about six or seven months, from August of 2011 to July of 2012, he had moved out and moved on, and I found myself in the midst of divorce. Since I previously had been a coach, I was familiar with the International Coach Federation (ICF) organization in my city; that's where I met Randy and Pegotty Cooper, the co-founders of CDC Certified Divorce Coach®. I took their course because I didn't want my ex to bully me in divorce court. I just really wanted to learn because that's my personality type. Once I went through my divorce and the CDC® course, I knew I wanted to help as many people as I possibly could through this difficult process.

Jeremy: Could you share more about the types of individuals you focus on and help? Is there a particular profile of your ideal client?

Pamela: My ideal client is somebody that not only wants to get over their divorce but is someone who wants to live their life to the fullest. They want to look at the concept of divorce not simply as a setback, but are willing to turn this setback into their major comeback and live their best life. It's somebody who can afford a coach, somebody who is positive, and who tries to take good care of themselves. That's both male and female.

A COMEBACK Roadmap Case Study: Belinda's Story

When Belinda initially approached me with tears in her eyes, she told me she that she needed to talk to me because she believed we had a lot in common, and she thought I could help her. Unfortunately, I knew exactly what she was feeling and where the direction her story was going. Her face said it all, and Belinda was wearing all the signs of a woman in pain.

Through her tears, she explained to me that her marriage of twenty years was ending, and she was entering into a new phase of her life. Belinda said she had been in her relationship for more than half her life, and she no longer knew who she was or where to go next. She felt numb and was having a hard time processing through the stages of divorce. She also explained to me she felt like she had lost her identity in her role as a wife and wasn't sure how to navigate her world without that title. Belinda explained that she was fearful of being a mother and quasi–father to her teenage sons.

She hired me as a coach at first to help her navigate through the initial phases of divorce and then to help her develop a new normal so that she could let go of what she had lost and move forward towards her new life as a single mother. I walked her through the COMEBACK process and we co-created new dreams and goals for her that represented who she was and where she wanted to go. We used her setback of divorce as the platform to launch her comeback.

Jeremy: Are your clients usually parents? Or do you help parents, as well as husbands and wives who don't have children?

Pamela: I work with both men and women. When I first got divorced and before I became a divorce coach I held the assumption that only women had gone through what I had been through. However, I now know after having many conversations with men and women I discovered that there are men who have had experiences similar to my own divorce. As a coach, I have met several single fathers who grapple with feelings of abandonment and rejection as well.

I prefer working with divorcing individuals who have children. My goal as a coach is to help my clients become the best versions of themselves while navigating through the divorce process. I particularly like working with parents who have children because it's even more important to be your best self, first for you and ultimately for your children.

Jeremy: Right. It's a whole a different kind of effort and a lot more work.

Pamela: Yes. Taking the high road is a must and living your best life takes on a whole new meaning for divorcing spouses with kids. That's my sweet spot.

Jeremy: You've talked about something called the COMEBACK Roadmap that you've created. What is the COMEBACK Roadmap?

Pamela: There are certain steps I think all people going through the divorce process need to walk through to get to where they want to be on the other side of divorce. I take them through the COMEBACK Roadmap steps,

"COMEBACK" is an acronym. It's not necessarily a linear process, just like the divorce process isn't linear, you ebb and flow through stages.

Choosing You

"**C**" stands for '**Choosing you.**' You have to focus on extreme self-care and choosing you to be your best self for your children and for the people you serve. Most of the time we put our kids and our spouse ahead of our self. During the coaching process, I teach them they now need to take good care of themselves so that they can feed people out of their overflow.

Obstacles

The second step, "**O**" stands for '**Obstacles**'. Many obstacles come with divorce. Some of them have to do with mindset, some of them are actual physical obstacles. So it could be financial stress, or it could be physical stress, or it could just be the fact that you've surrounded yourself with negative people, or you have negative thinking.

Make the Declaration

The next step, "**M**" stands for '**Make the declaration**', or 'Just Do It', like Nike says. Decide that you're going to do it and then declare that you are going to make a comeback.

Embrace Chaos

"**E**" stands for '**Embrace chaos**,' because with divorce and with change, there's going to be many levels of chaos. It's almost like when you renovate a house, you have to gut it a little bit in certain places, pull things out, and it gets messy and dusty before you can start over with something new.

Believe

The next phase, "**B**" stands for '**Believe**'. Sometimes when you're going through a divorce, it's hard to believe that you're going to be able to get to where you want to be because it can be long, and similar to the stages of grief, you go in and out of them.

Adjust & Adapt

"**A**" is make sure you '**Adjust & Adapt**' and become resilient in the process.

Communicate

The next step, "**C**" stands for '**Communicate**'. There's communication on many levels. It's what you say to yourself - you may have negative messages that are on a constant loop. It's what you say to others, your nonverbal communication. It's how you present yourself to the world, your interpersonal communication. As well as how you communicate with your children and your ex-spouse. I help them focus on all levels of communication.

Keep on Moving

Lastly, "**K**" is for '**Keep on Moving**'. Keep on moving, keep on taking action, keep on believing, keep on loving, keep on communicating well, and keep on forgiving, because forgiveness is a huge piece in the process.

The COMEBACK Roadmap Steps

C: Choosing You

O: Overcome obstacles

M: Make a declaration

E: Embrace chaos

B: Believe

A: Adjust and Adapt

C: Communication

K: Keep moving

A COMEBACK Roadmap Case Study: Margareet's Story

When I began working with Margareet, she was still very traumatized by her divorce and custody case. She was in a lot of pain, and she was still stuck in her story. From our initial coaching session, Margareet knew she needed to take her eyes off of her ex-husband and his new wife and life and focus on moving towards her future. At the time, she had spent the past five years fighting for custody, which she had recently been granted.

I walked her through the COMEBACK process. We first discussed ways she could honor and love herself again. I believe it is impossible to love someone else if you don't love yourself. We co-created self-honoring strategies and a few things that she would focus on to take good care of herself. She chose to drink her favorite cup of tea and to resume a writing career that she had given up years ago.

Another place she devoted her attention to was the way she was communicating to herself and others. She was stuck in her story, and she would frequently refer to it although she had been divorced for several years. We created an alternative way of thinking about her story and how she communicated to herself when she fell into a negative dialogue. We worked on reframing her story to reflect the wonderful vibrant story she was now creating. For example, when we first started working together she felt like her ex and his new wife were living in this great world and how she felt "Her life sucked!" We developed a dialogue that she would recite every time she saw herself sinking into that mindset that stated that she was free to design the type of life for herself and her daughter, free from distraction and compromise. Her life could be whatever she wanted it to be going forward. By changing her intra-personal communication (what she said to herself), her outlook completely changed.

Finally, we worked on keeping her moving forward. There were two areas where she believed she needed to focus. One, staying in a constant state of forgiveness. First, for herself, because she was stuck in a loop of feeling like she had done something wrong by picking the wrong person and she kept blaming herself for the demise of her relationship. We worked on not focusing or blaming herself or anyone else and on forgiving herself and looking at the great outcome of the relationship which was her beautiful daughter. Finally, she focused on forgiving her ex-husband and his wife so that they could successfully co-parent their child as a blended family. We both agreed that the negative emotions did nothing to support the new normal and new person she had now become.

Jeremy: Now walk us through a typical early coaching session with somebody that you work with.

Pamela: An initial coaching session is the discovery phase. I want to find out where the person is. I want to get an idea of how they're feeling and what their ultimate outcomes are. In this discovery phase, I ask several questions to find out who they are, where they are, and where they want to focus on the divorce process. Because there is a beginning phase, there's the actual divorce process phase, and then there's the phase where you're moving on. I want to find out exactly where they are and find out as much information as I can. Then the client and I co-create a process so that they can get to their ultimate outcomes.

Jeremy: What would you say are the most common challenges that someone may have when going through a divorce?

Pamela: One challenge is fear because they're often wondering what's going to become of them after divorce. A lot of times, they have negative belief systems that tell them they're never going to survive or never going to meet anyone. Also, another enormous challenge they often face is moving on from an anger phase. A common misconception they often have deals with communicating with their legal professionals. Divorce can be very expensive, but if you remain calm in the process and collect your thoughts before you call your attorney, it can save you probably 50-60% of the cost.

You can also look at the alternative, non-traditional ways of handling your divorce.

Jeremy: The feeling of having to 'go it alone' is a common misconception that people often have when going through their divorce. How do you help them dispel this misconception and help them understand they can go through their divorce with the support they need?

Pamela: That's an excellent question because I think that has a lot to do with this mindset shift. Many people do feel like they have to 'go it alone.' I know even in my situation, I felt like I was surrounded in suburbia with all these intact two-parent homes. That's not necessarily true. You can help them explore other ways, such as finding other women or men going through a divorce, find divorce support groups, as well as find a divorce coach to help them go through the process. It's just by shifting their thought process from "I am alone" to "These are all my options." That's what I try to get my clients to understand.

Jeremy: Can you share with us a story of a client you've worked with who was going through some rough patches? Perhaps they were feeling alone and overwhelmed, but by applying insights they gained from working with you, they were able to overcome those challenges and fears and emerge from their divorce in a place where they were happy and emotionally healthy?

Pamela: Yes. One of the women I coached who was one of my earlier clients which I've continued to work with over the years, first came to me completely overwhelmed. When we first started working together, she did not have a job. She had two small children. One of them was three, and the other one was probably in the second grade. She had just overcome a painful divorce. Her husband had abused her, and that was the last straw in her divorce scenario. The floor was entirely pulled out of her life, and she had to restructure and regain a whole new life.

We started out with creating a vision that she wanted to have for her future. We went through all of the scenarios in which she was able to do what she set out to do. Then we created a framework to help her get on track. She had three phases we needed to get through. These three phases consisted of the parenting phase, the job phase, and the getting herself together phase. We took them step by step and helped her create winning environments as a parent, established an excellent support network, and created a winning environment to help her get back on track with getting a job. Now she's gainfully employed and has been for the past five years. The last phase of the process was about finding love again, and now she is in a committed, wonderful relationship. She worked on herself first, along with her parenting, next she improved her job situation, then she found love again.

Jeremy: If you're going to crystallize the key benefit, or key opportunity for growth, after going through this work, what would you identify that as?

Pamela: The key is to identify opportunities in divorce for taking the high road. You can be tempted to stay in a negative place or rehearse old stories that aren't necessarily true, but taking the high road is looking at the bright side of every situation and being cognizant of every choice you make during the divorce process. Acknowledge and get support when and where you need it, and then use the support to help you get back on track.

Jeremy: In closing, what's one of the most important things that people should consider when they're going through a divorce?

Pamela: The main thing to consider is that you're not alone, and you will get through it, many people have, and that this is not necessarily a negative thing. You get a chance to create a whole brand-new life for yourself that includes joy and freedom. I would look at it like that, and that's probably one of the best ways of shifting from divorce to a new great life.

Jeremy: Thanks for the great wisdom and words of advice, Pamela. As we close, how can someone find out more about you?

Pamela: I can be contacted at www.PamelaDykes.com or check out my blog called "The Comeback Mom Lab."

Key Takeaways

√   **Stay calm.**

√   **Take it one day at a time.**

√   **Begin with the end in mind.**

√   **Everyone can and will make a Comeback.**

ABOUT PAMELA Y. DYKES, Ph.D., CDC®, ACC, MCM, FLORIDA SUPREME COURT CERTIFIED FAMILY MEDIATOR

Pamela Dykes is an author, speaker, and coach who specializes is helping men and women tap into their greatest potential and turn perceived setbacks into compelling comebacks to reach their full potential. Her passion for helping people through life's difficult transitions began when she found herself in the midst of an identity crisis where she desperately wanted to regain control of her personal life and career.

However, her comeback journey was further complicated by the devastating impact of divorce. Using her unique success journey, background as a communication expert, professional coach training, and hands-on work with 100's of individuals she has developed a clear understanding of the necessary steps one needs to take to turn all life's setbacks into comebacks. This resulted in the development of her unique system: The COMEBACK Road Map, a specific set of steps that include extreme self-care, strategies to overcome obstacles and necessary habits and skills needed for personal transformation.

BUSINESS: PD Coaching

WEBSITE: www.PamelaDykes.com

BLOG: www.thecomebackmomlab.com

EMAIL: info@PamelaDykes.com

PHONE: 813.751.5864

LOCATION: Tampa, FL

CHAPTER SEVEN

DIVORCING WITH DIGNITY

Interview with **Lisa M. McNally** CDC Certified

Divorce Coach® & Certified Family (Divorce) Mediator

> *"We must be willing to let go of the life we've planned, so as to have the life that is waiting for us." — Joseph Campbell*

Jeremy: Lisa can you tell me about "Changing Times Mediation and Best Interest Coaching" as well as your roles of divorce mediator and divorce coach?

Lisa: As a divorce mediator I work with couples to reach mutually acceptable agreements in a confidential, individualized, self-determining and less time-consuming and expensive way in which they, not the court, control the decisions that affect their family, their finances, their business and their lives.

I serve as a neutral third party who doesn't take anyone's side in the divorce. My role is to help the parties communicate effectively with each other to facilitate discussions so they can reach well thought out agreements. I assist both sides in identifying the issues that must be resolved before they can dissolve their marriage in their state. I also help with additional issues they wish to include; identifying and discussing viable options to resolve their problems; clearly defining their agreements, and keeping them focused on the issues at hand throughout the process.

The outcome of their work with me is a Mediated Agreement that contains the agreements they reached in the mediation process which they want the overseeing court to approve and incorporate into the court's Decree of Divorce.

As a divorce coach, I work with just one of the individuals involved in a divorce. In this role, I work one-on-one with my client helping them to navigate their way through the overwhelm and stress that's often part of a divorce. My client receives support from me in managing aspects of their divorce that don't require legal advice. This would include helping them develop and utilize skills necessary to minimize the stress associated with their divorce and maximize their ability to achieve their divorce-related goals.

Throughout the coaching process, I help my clients learn how to effectively:

- Become and remain resilient

- Advocate for themselves and their children throughout the divorce process and beyond

- Identify and communicate their needs, wants and desires in an effective way

- Communicate with the other parties involved in their divorce including their spouse, attorney, and other professionals

- Manage conflict in a positive way

- Get and remain organized

- Make informed decisions

- Identify and set goals

- Prioritize and complete the many tasks related to their divorce within the timelines provided

- Employ time management techniques

- Identify, seek and secure professional services when deemed necessary

- Maintain a future focus on what's important to them, what's in their best interest and what's in their children's best interest

Jeremy: How did you get started in divorce mediation & divorce coaching?

Lisa: My interest in becoming a divorce mediator began in the late 1990's during my career as a family law paralegal. In that role, I assisted a family law attorney in litigating all aspects of divorces through the court system and witnessed how incredibly costly and destructive that approach was on the individuals involved in the divorce, including their children and other family members. I found the adverse effects of the court process on their parenting relationships, finances, emotional well-being and futures to be barbaric, long-lasting and avoidable under different circumstances, such as divorce mediation.

My desire to help minimize the negative effects of divorce on individuals, children and families inspired me to pursue becoming a divorce mediator. Since that time, I've successfully helped hundreds of families mediate all aspects of their divorces in a confidential, respectful and dignified manner without the need for court involvement in the decision-making process.

I became a divorce coach to broaden my ability to help people experiencing and affected by divorce. As a divorce coach, I'm able to help individuals that, for whatever reason, aren't candidates for mediation but can still benefit from having someone help them navigate their way through the often complicated journey of their divorce.

I really can't say enough about how incredibly effective mediation is for couples and divorce coaching is for individuals. And the benefits to any children involved are immeasurable.

Jeremy: What are some of the most common obstacles or misconceptions divorcing couples have with both the divorce mediation and coaching process?

Lisa: Those are different for mediation and divorce coaching.

Mediation Misconceptions

The most common fear people have about the mediation process is that they don't know what they don't know, especially about their finances. Often in a relationship, the parties divvy up various marital responsibilities such as child-rearing and family finances with one of them taking the lead on managing those and the other typically being informed but not intimately aware of all of the details. This leads to the misconception that the currently informed party will have the upper-hand in the mediation process. This isn't the case because the mediation process involves full disclosure and thorough information sharing about all aspects of their lives including finances and children.

Divorce Coaching Misconceptions

With coaching, I would say that the most common misconception people have is that coaching is the same as therapy. For that reason, those individuals already partaking in therapy may avoid divorce coaching because they think it will duplicate the service and support they're already receiving. For individuals who aren't in therapy because they don't believe they can benefit from therapy, may also think they can't benefit from coaching if they feel they are essentially the same thing. The misconception here is that therapy and coaching are one in the same. They are actually very different in nature and have their own important roles in the loves of people affected by divorce.

Jeremy: How do you help a client overcome fear in the mediation process and can you explain in more detail the differences between coaching and therapy?

Lisa: Once engaged in the mediation process the parties' concerns and fears about the unknown are quickly alleviated when they learn that the process of mediation includes both sides becoming familiar with all aspects of the family finances and other details of their relationship issues before discussing them, identifying possible solutions and reaching agreements.

Although there are some areas of overlap with divorce coaching and therapy, they are unique in nature, focus, and outcome and therefore are two very different professions.

Divorce Coaching -vs- Therapy

Some of the critical differences between divorce coaching and therapy are:

- A divorce coach's focus is on evolving and manifesting their client's potential whereas a therapist's focus is on healing and understanding.

- A divorce coach's emphasis is on the present and future, whereas a therapist's focus is on the past and present.

- A divorce coach is action-, being- and solution-oriented, whereas a therapist is problem-oriented.

- A divorce coach explores actions and behaviors that manifest high self-esteem, whereas a therapist explores the genesis of behaviors that create low self-esteem.

- A divorce coach and client answer the question "What's next? What now?" whereas a therapist and client answer the question, "Why and from where?"

- A divorce coach works mainly with external issues, whereas a therapist works primarily with internal issues.

- A divorce coach uses coaching skills, whereas a therapist uses therapy techniques.

Jeremy: Lisa please share with us the most important things to consider in mediation and divorce coaching?

Most Important Considerations in Mediation

Lisa: Although there are many benefits couples experience when they mediate rather than litigate - including the process being less expensive and time-consuming than litigation - I believe the most valuable and important benefit is the fact that they, not the court, attorneys or other professionals make the decisions that affect them and their children. They maintain control over making the decisions that affect their lives.

Most Important Considerations in Divorce Coaching

Clients who are coached during their divorce benefit greatly from having someone with the knowledge and expertise to help them through all aspects of their divorce journey. A divorce coach is someone who bridges the gap between their emotional needs and their legal needs. It is someone who understands and can help them move through their difficult present with a focus on the future they want for themselves and their children. A divorce coach is someone who believes in their client and helps them believe in themselves.

Jeremy: I understand that you're a licensed Real Estate Broker with many years of experience in real estate transactions including non-distressed sales as well as distressed sales such as those that involve divorces, short sales, and foreclosures. Can you tell me how your real estate training and experience benefits your divorce mediation and coaching clients?

Lisa: Yes. My real estate training and experience have proven to be incredibly valuable to my clients. For most couples, the largest, most valuable asset they possess is their marital home and thus what happens with it can have a significant impact on their finances in many different ways. Additionally, it's often understandably one of the most difficult topics for people to discuss because they view their home as their safe place that they created for their family, and the thought of losing it in addition to their marriage can sometimes be overwhelming and unbearable.

My years of real estate training and experience enable me to help the people I'm working with have meaningful and productive discussions about the various options that may be available to them regarding their real estate. I help them identify the options that are most desirable and viable to them and assist them in troubleshooting those options while keeping everyone's best interest in mind. And ultimately define the terms and conditions of the option they deem to be the best for them and their children.

These discussions are very sensitive in nature but critical to my client's ongoing well-being, both financially and emotionally. They require specific expertise and knowledge to successfully outline the steps to be taken to transition them into their new living situations and lives. My real estate background enables me to help my clients reach agreements that are tailored to their specific needs and abilities which have been invaluable.

Jeremy: Thanks for your insights Lisa. How can someone find out more about you and your divorce mediation and coaching business?

Lisa: I invite anyone to reach out to me confidentially in whatever way is most comfortable to them; phone, e-mail or my website.

They can schedule a free, no-obligation consultation and on my website they can receive my "10 Critical Steps to Prepare for Divorce". I offer in-person consultations to those who can meet with me in person as well as consultations via Skype and phone.

My services are not limited by geographical location; I can work with people in all states.

Key Takeaways

√   **Mediation works!**

√   **Coaching is empowering and uplifting**

√   **Divorce doesn't have to destroy families.**

√   **Children benefit when parents, not courts, decide their futures.**

√   **Divorce can be alienating…You don't have to go it alone.**

ABOUT LISA M. MCNALLY, CDC Certified Divorce Coach® & Certified Family (Divorce) Mediator

Lisa McNally, entrepreneur, professional, and, most importantly, mother of three, has 20+ years of experience working with divorcing individuals, couples and families in all aspects of family law matters including divorce, separation, child custody, co-parenting and parental rights. Lisa's first-hand experience with the personal, familial, psychological and financial destruction divorce frequently has on families is what fueled her desire to help minimize and potentially eliminate the damage families experience.

As a Divorce Mediator, Lisa has been helping couples for decades reach agreements on all aspects of their divorce and other family law matters outside of the Court process. She is known for compassionately and skillfully assisting families in reaching fair, family-focused, child-centered agreements with a focus on the best interest of all children involved.

As a Divorce Coach, Lisa supports and guides individuals experiencing divorce one-on-one, helping them navigate the often lengthy, stressful and convoluted process in a dignified way. Her clients benefit by having her by their side to help them make the best possible decisions for themselves and their children based on their unique interests, needs, concerns, and goals. Lisa is dedicated to helping the parents and children she works with live happy, healthy, secure and fulfilling lives.

BUSINESS: Best Interest Coaching & Changing Times Mediation

WEBSITE: www.BestInterestCoaching.com & www.ChangingTimesMediation.com

EMAIL: LisaMcNally2015@gmail.com

PHONE: 603.617.0806

CHAPTER EIGHT

BEING THE CAPTAIN OF YOUR DIVORCE TEAM

Interview with **Marie Marhan Dropkin**, CDC®

> *"If you don't remain the captain of your divorce team, someone else will be making life altering decisions for you. Is that what you really want?"* — *Marie Marhan Dropkin*

Jeremy: Marie, can there be a simple strategy to get you through your divorce? And can you really take the high road, when you're at your lowest? Is a healthy divorce possible?

Marie: Yes, it is. But not without conscious thought and intentional decision-making.

When you have a simple strategy to get through divorce, or any strategy, it means you have thought, "How am I going to get from here, to there? What outcome do I really want for the immediate future? For the long term?" It is so easy to get caught up in the drama of what is unfolding that you lose sight of what is truly important in the long run. No one consciously says, "Gee, I'd like to have a nasty divorce, where we always exchange snarky comments and try to make our children hate their other parent." Or, "I'd like to model terrible partner behavior, so my child never wants to be in a relationship, get married or become a parent." How about: "I want every future event in my child's life to be awkward, for all of us, especially them: their school events, graduations, weddings, and own children's births." Neither do people wish to come out of divorce financially ruined or facing poverty for their children, or with their self-esteem devastated to the point they feel no one will ever give them a second look again. If you want to avoid those outcomes, there is help.

Jeremy: What do we mean by "Taking the High Road?"

Marie: When you take "the High Road," you conduct yourself using superior moral standards, doing the right thing even during difficult circumstances. If you want to feel you did the best you could during your divorce, you must be your "best self," and maintain your dignity as well as you can. You will have the rest of your life to look back and second guess your actions and decisions that you made during this challenging time.

There are always many approaches to any situation: from reacting impulsively driven by your emotions, to calming down and thinking rationally before responding. You must make the conscious choice that you want the best outcome possible: a healthy divorce. A divorce you feel, well, maybe not happy about, but one where you are confident you did your best for all involved to rise above unpleasantness so that relationships are not horribly damaged in the process. A healthy divorce. How do some people get that?

Think, first, about what dignity means. It's how you feel about yourself, and your sense of how others perceive you. Many things change with the onset of divorce, whether we welcome them or not. Your sense of new independence may be anxiety-provoking, whether in the financial, parenting or relationship areas. Your self-perception of value as a partner, your sense of "lovability," may have been shaken by this failed marriage. To come through divorce with dignity intact, knowing you were your "best self" throughout, depends on adjustment to these changes through thought and planning.

Jeremy: Can you share a little bit about your divorce coaching practice, Support in a Storm, and what types of people that you help?

Marie: I named the business Support in a Storm because I wanted a name that would convey a safe place during a difficult time. The logo for my company shows two people walking together underneath an umbrella through a rainstorm. This image appealed to me because one person is holding the umbrella in that situation and protecting the other person from the storm, from the rain. I liked that feeling of...'I will walk through this difficult time with you and help you get through it unscathed'.

That's the history of the naming of my business and that's what I try to do with my divorce coaching practice. I try to champion people through difficult times and help them get through it as best as possible.

Step 1: Educate Yourself

Jeremy: I like that, more like a tropical storm instead of a harsh winter storm or snowstorm.

Can you share with us what inspired you to enter this field and become a divorce coach?

Marie: Well, I went through a tough divorce a few years back, and I watched several friends and acquaintances make terrible mistakes when they went through their divorces, choices they made that affected them for the rest of their lives because they couldn't undo them. Some just got worn down by the pressure, and they gave in to less than they deserved, just to have it be over. Also, just the decisions that I watched them make weren't what they wanted. When I knew it was time for me to get divorced, I said, "That's not going to be me."

I started reading everything I could get my hands on. The library's a great resource because you don't need to spend money. I was downloading eBooks and other information so that I could learn everything I needed to know and be able to judge whether I was making good decisions or not. I even told my friends that I was getting a master's degree in divorce because I was spending so much time educating myself. It's hard to focus when you're under stress to this level, but I knew that this was my one opportunity to get it right, and I wanted to do the very best job I could.

After my divorce, I looked back and realized I had learned a great deal from the experience. I wanted to help other people going through divorce because it's such a vulnerable time. I wanted to help them know they don't have to go through it alone like I did. That's why I got started in this field.

Jeremy: You say that one of your primary goals when working with clients going through a divorce is to help them maintain dignity through the process.

What may I ask are the most common challenges or maybe the misconceptions that people have when going through a divorce; specifically, what inhibits people from being able to emerge from the divorce process with their dignity intact?

Marie: People are so emotional when they're going through their divorce. They're not thinking straight, and their emotions can run away with them. It's a challenge to make good logical decisions when you're in such an altered state. For somebody to come out of their divorce with their dignity intact, I think this means to feel that you did the very best you could for yourself, and behaved the very best you could during that emotional time. To avoid making the mistakes, people need to focus on: 'How am I going to do the best I can and be my best advocate?'

Step 2: Use Care When Building Your Team

Having a "Divorce Team" is perhaps a surprise because people think that when they go to an attorney and give them a lot of money, that the lawyer's going to take over and run the whole divorce and take care of everything. Sometimes an attorney wants you to think that. One lawyer I interviewed told me he was going to take care of me, and I didn't have to worry. He wanted to make me feel safe, and it was very believable.

Honestly, all the attorneys that you interview want your business and anybody who wants your business is going to be putting their best face forward, telling you what they think you want to hear, so that you will sign on with them. The truth is that most lawyers didn't go into law so that they could listen to your heartbreaking story or give you financial advice or refer you to another divorce professional. Your attorney is a specialist who deals with the business of you getting divorced, so they're excellent at that.

For the other pieces of the divorce that are going to come your way, you need other players on your team. To be your best advocate, you need to construct your team of divorce professionals so that you can get the help you need from all different areas.

Jeremy: That's a great point, the attorneys are in the business of divorce, right? They're going to say what you think you want to hear while you're in a vulnerable state. You have to be cautious of that. We know that people with high degrees of empathy don't necessarily go into the law profession, and a law school doesn't exactly nurture or encourage empathy. It's more of a dispassionate process of following the letter of the law and procedure and everything else along those lines.

Marie: Nor would you want to rely on your attorney as that compassionate person because you're hiring them for a particular purpose, plus paying $300-$400 an hour to a lawyer vs. utilizing other types of support people, doesn't make any sense. Those are some excellent points.

Step 3: Remain the Captain of Your Team

Nobody's going to care as much as you do about the outcome of your divorce. You have to be the captain of your team. You need to be your best advocate.

Jeremy: Marie, tell me how you would advise someone going through divorce on how best to take back the reins, and become captain of their team, their best advocate?

Marie: To be your best advocate, you need to be able to speak for yourself and to do that you need to educate yourself, so you know what you're talking about. Then nobody's going to bamboozle you or give you wrong information. You'll be able to judge and weigh it yourself.

The second piece of that is getting professional advice from divorce experts.

You need that to get that expert advice if you don't feel comfortable in that arena. Whether it's a therapist, an accountant, or somebody who's trained in financial advising for divorce specifically. The third thing I'd say is, remember that you're in control. Stay in charge and make the decisions, don't let people make decisions for you or push you into agreeing to things that aren't what you want. The last thing I feel strongly about is keeping the big picture in mind. You want to think about how your life is going to be ten years from now.

Step 4: Keep the Big Picture in Mind

This is where a Divorce Coach can help from beginning to end. A divorce coach can assist you as a thinking partner when your reactions are centered in your knee-jerk emotional responses that vent your stress and increase the friction when it's hard to process logically. They can help you keep your goal in mind: the goal of the best possible outcome for you and your children: a healthy divorce.

You don't want things to get so nasty and unpleasant that ten years from now when you're celebrating your child's high school graduation or wedding, it is awkward for you or your child. You want to keep relationships with your ex-spouse and extended relatives the best you possibly can, do the best you can to remain unemotional. It's hard, but just keep that picture in mind. Think of how it is going to be when you're in a different place down the road when you have to interact after having been through this difficult time. Keep that in the back of your mind so that you can get there and be on the best terms possible.

Jeremy: It's almost like mental role-playing, right? Imagining yourself in that situation and how you would react and anticipate how you might react.

Marie: Yes, you know they say if you believe or can see a picture of yourself when you're retired, it helps people save for retirement. In this case, I'm suggesting that if you can see yourself ten years after the divorce, how do you want to be getting along with the ex-spouse? What you do now will set up the groundwork for the relationship you'll have then. It's not easy, because if both people don't keep that in mind, you won't be very likely to get there.

Even suggest this to your divorcing spouse, help them to imagine ten years from now, how you want to be able to be sitting at the same table at your child's special life event. We want to keep that in our heads while we're going through this. It's not all about the intense emotions that we're having right now.

Jeremy: Of course, it is optimal if both parties are on the same page regarding that visualization, looking out five, ten years from now, although that's not always necessarily possible. I suppose the person that's least cooperative is going to have the tendency to bring the ship down, so you're trying to bring the ship back and trying to take the high road and maintain focus on the positivity.

Marie: Right. Keeping that in mind will help you maintain your dignity throughout the divorce because you'll act on what's best for the long haul, not what feels good in the immediate moment.

Jeremy: I know every divorce coach has been shaped by their life experiences, and they have their biases and perspectives, do you have suggestions on how people can find the right one for themselves?

Marie: Most divorce coaches have experienced different kinds of clients, but there's a commonality in that people going through divorce are in shock. They are emotional; they are trying to process all types of tasks that need to get done, maybe when they're hysterical or grieving their situation and the loss. Even if they chose a divorce, it's not what they wanted and pictured for their lives. Any divorce coach would be able to help any person, I think, going through divorce.

Some do specialize in certain areas or types of clients, like people with young children. Some, like myself, have exited a long-term marriage, so my personal experience is stronger in that area. I would try and help any person who wanted my help getting through their divorce and making decisions and processing everything that goes along with it.

Jeremy: Now can you share with us a story of a client you're worked with who was going through some rough patches. Maybe they were facing some significant challenges, felt pretty helpless, but by applying the insights they gained from working with you they were able to overcome their challenges and fears and emerge from the divorce in a place where they were happy and emotionally healthy? They came out with their dignity intact.

Marie: One simple story comes to mind which highlights how sidetracked people can get when they're in an emotional state, in which one detail can seem so blown out of proportion. I had a client who was just beside herself with anxiety. She wanted to leave her husband; she was in a very abusive situation, and very fearful of his reaction when she told him she wanted a divorce. But there were certain situations at play, individual factors that made it in her best interests to delay for a few months before asking for a divorce, even though mentally she was ready.

She was so fixated on a particular date because their lease for their home they were renting was coming due and she just had convinced herself that date was the day she had to tell him that she wanted a divorce, even though it wasn't a good time in the big picture. Just by talking and listening to her, I realized she was overlooking the fact that she could delay that date just by talking to her landlord. Perhaps asking for an extension, maybe going month-to-month for a few months and thereby buy herself some time to calm down, have a good plan in place and also to meet a deadline that was in her benefit to reach.

Just helping her focus on getting an extension on the lease became the next step, not the overwhelming task of telling her husband she wanted a divorce. That relieved a lot of pressure. She then had the time she needed to be mentally ready to approach him about a divorce. That's just a small piece but just factors like that, get people so sidetracked with hysteria that they can't move forward. They can't make a good decision about the next step. That's where a divorce coach like myself will benefit them.

Jeremy: What's one of the most important things you think people should consider when they're going through a divorce?

Marie: I think they need to know that no matter how terrible they feel right now they will get through this. It's one of the most stressful things you'll experience in your life, but you will survive, and you will be happy again. You might be surprised at how happy you can be by just getting through this part, it will happen, and sometimes people lose sight of that. They think they're never going to feel any differently than they feel right at that moment, so I just want to reassure everybody listening that you will get through your divorce.

Jeremy: Perfect, thank you so much, Marie, I appreciate all your insights. In closing, can you share how someone can find out more about you and how to contact you in your business?

Marie: The best way to contact me is through my website: www.supportinastorm.com or via email marie@SupportInAStorm.com. I'm also available via phone at 518.423.2525.

I offer an initial complimentary session to help people focus forward and think about the next step. This is especially helpful for somebody who's at the very beginning of a divorce. They may not know what to do first, and may be feeling overwhelmed. There's no obligation for that initial session.

I also have several lists available; one is about choosing an attorney, the questions to ask, and things to think about while you're interviewing lawyers. Readers are welcome to check the website and email me requesting a specific list.

Key Takeaways

For a healthy divorce:

√   **Get prepared for your divorce.**

√   **Act as your best self.**

√   **Build your team carefully.**

√   **Remain the captain of your team.**

√   **Keep the big picture in mind.**

ABOUT MARIE MARHAN DROPKIN, CDC®

After a decades-long marriage and raising four great kids, Marie faced a complicated divorce. Watching other women make mistakes they regretted for the rest of their lives inspired her to become her own best advocate. Marie read everything she could get her hands on regarding divorce, and told friends she was getting a "master's degree in divorce!"

She emerged stronger and wiser and wanting to help others survive their divorces emotionally and financially intact. CDC® Divorce Coach training further expanded on what she'd learned in her personal experience, adding to professional degrees in Pharmacy, Religious Studies, Bereavement Studies and Life Coaching. Years of training and working as a hospital chaplain, listening and companioning people through the worst crises life has to offer gave Marie the skills to help you face whatever your divorce has brought you.

BUSINESS: Support In A Storm

WEBSITE: www.SupportInAStorm.com

EMAIL: marie@SupportInAStorm.com

PHONE: 518.423.2525

LOCATION: Delmar, NY

LINKEDIN: www.linkedin.com/in/marie-marhan-dropkin-984678b4

CHAPTER NINE

SELF-EMPOWERMENT THROUGH DECISION-MAKING

Interview with **Tracy Callahan,** MA, CDC®

> *"By engaging in effective decision-making that is consistent with your values, personal interests, and authentic self, you are taking the action necessary to positively and amicably move toward an agreement in your divorce."* — Tracy Callahan

Jeremy: Tracy, today you're going to talk to us about self-empowerment through effective decision-making, moving from action to agreement in the divorce process. Could you share a little bit about your background and how you got into this field?

Tracy: I am a CDC Certified Divorce Coach® as well as a Florida Certified Family Mediator. I began my career in mediation approximately seven years ago in New York City after leaving a long career in the healthcare industry as an administrator and executive. Recognizing how very stressful and destructive conflict can be for most individuals, personally and professionally, I became an advocate of Alternative Dispute Resolution (ADR) processes. In other words, I wanted to help people in conflict find other ways to deal with their problems without resorting to verbal and physical fighting. Intrigued with conflict, my work as a mediator and conflict coach provided me with the opportunity to educate individuals about conflict responses as well as support them in a facilitative manner, providing forums and opportunities to resolve their conflicts and move forward, together or apart, in a positive manner.

After leaving New York City and moving to Palm Beach County five years ago, I became a Supreme Court of Florida Certified Family Mediator and opened my own practice, Mediating-Matters, LLC. Focusing all of my energy on family and divorce mediation, I was surprised by the number of potential clients who reached out to me initially seeking information about mediation but were really in search of a supportive individual to help them through the process of their divorce. These potential clients shared very similar qualities and feelings of being alone, confused and certainly overwhelmed by the thought of their own divorce. Recognizing my limitations to support and advocate for these individuals as a neutral facilitator and mediator, I began looking for and sought out the practice of divorce coaching through the CDC® program, the only certifying program for divorce coaches in the United States, to compliment my offerings as a divorce professional.

As a divorce coach, with the experience as a mediator, I am able to effectively work with my clients in an honest and supportive manner to handle the business of divorce including:

- getting organized

- clarifying needs

- choosing a court process that best suits them and their partner preparing for the process

- parenting plans

- property division

- asset and debt allocation

- financial management

- making effective decisions

- eventually reaching an agreement or settlement

While simultaneously working with my clients in addressing the internal work needed throughout the various stages of the divorce process including:

- emotional management

- acceptance

- letting go

- forgiveness

- happiness

- being true to their "Best Self"

Working with many clients over the years as a Certified Divorce Coach, I am passionate about supporting individuals through the divorce process and believe that the secret to moving forward in a healthy and peaceful way is through the skill development and practice of empowered and informed decision-making that reflects their best interest as well as the best interest of their families. With the goal of empowering, growing and developing, I truly believe that divorce can be an opportunity, not a tragedy. Not an ending but a beginning. As such, a great deal of my specialty work has been with women in their 40's who have left their professional careers to raise and nurture their families, been out of the workforce for many years, and now find themselves in the process of getting divorced and re-entering the workforce as a newly single individual and full time working mom. Supporting these women to amicably end their marriage, redefine themselves and their family, find a fulfilling job, and start on the road to independence has been one of the most meaningful and rewarding aspects of my career.

Jeremy: You talk a lot about self-empowerment through effective decision-making. Share with us why decision-making in divorce can be very difficult.

Tracy: I hear from my clients all the time, divorce is one of the hardest decisions they ever had to make or face. Whether contemplating getting divorced or responding to a divorce, you are embarking on a journey that can be unknown, scary, and difficult. But, that journey doesn't necessarily have to be filled with given conflict and uncertainty. And, it certainly doesn't need to be alone. It does, however, require lots of decisions to be made and those decisions can be anything from "should I keep the marital home" to "what do I want my life to be like when this is all over"?

To begin with, decision-making in divorce is a process that involves many different factors.

Decision-Making Factors

Time

In divorce, people are immediately thrown into a process where decisions need to be made and it can feel extremely pressured. Divorce requires us to make decisions when we feel less equipped to do so with really big stakes. Even though we make decisions every single day of our lives, like what will we eat for breakfast or what time will we wake up, divorce is very different.

Emotions

Second, decision-making in divorce can be emotionally charged, filled with lots of emotional pain and anguish. Out of fear, one can avoid or remove themselves entirely from the decision-making process often leaving them more vulnerable and out of control.

Transition

Third, divorce is a time of transition where you may find yourself re-defining almost everything you know or what you use to know. This can include family, friends, in-laws, housing, finances and your overall well-being. This transition further complicates the decision-making process as there is no longer a norm to base or evaluate your decisions upon.

Jeremy: In the context of divorce, what kind of decisions do people need to make?

Tracy: In divorce, the list of things that need to be decided can be overwhelming, to say the least. Decisions ranging from how to tell the children to what legal process is best for me and my family are just the beginning. Typically, I get asked big encompassing questions like, "what do I do now?" and "what are my options?" These are process questions that commonly refer to handling the legality of divorce and are usually the first most important step in the decision-making process as they can greatly impact the outcome of the divorce.

There are many options available to individuals in most states when it comes to pursuing divorce including, but not limited to:

- trial in court

- attorney representation

- mediation

- Pro-Se representation and mediation

- collaborative divorce

- or a hybrid model comprising of a combination of two of these

Working with someone who has an understanding of these options and or educating yourself as to the laws applicable to your state, is essential. Most state's judicial systems have websites sharing information about divorce and the divorce process for your reference.

Three Main Divorce Decision-Making Categories

Once a process decision has been made, most other decisions that need to be made in the divorce, typically fall into three main categories:

1. **Parenting-Visitation**

Who lives where, with who and when, and how decisions will be made on behalf of the children (including education, healthcare, and religion).

2. **Asset, Debt and Property Division**

Division of marital assets, debts, and property, as well as the determination of non-marital property.

3. **Financial Support**

Child Support and / or Spousal Maintenance.

Jeremy: Divorce is a very stressful time. It can be very overwhelming, and there's a lot of pressure to make the right decision. Can you share a little bit more about that process for your clients?

Tracy: The landscape of divorce is interesting because it's multi-layered and often very difficult to navigate. It's a time of change and transition where we find ourselves redefining everything that we knew to be true. Whether that's our family, our friends, our housing or our finances. It's also a very intense emotional time where there are lots of feelings like denial, shame, anger, frustration, and helplessness. Then, all of that is coupled with the legal process that has its own language, intricacies, difficulties, and stressors. It is no wonder that people facing divorce have a difficult time engaging in the decision-making process.

No matter how amazing and prepared you are, the reality is, it is an extremely difficult task to make one decision let alone lots of decisions when you or your family are working from a place of stress, pressure, or fear of the unknown. I, however, strongly believe, based upon the work I have done with numerous clients, that engaging in the decision-making process rather than avoiding it or handing it over to someone else, actually minimizes the stress and fear and enhances your confidence, strength, and independence. By exerting a level of control over your own life, the decision-making process becomes a vehicle to help you achieve your goals.

Five Cognitive Decision-Making Process Steps in Divorce

Decision-making is a cognitive process that requires a certain set of steps. These steps include:

1. **Setting goals**

What is it that you have to decide? What priority is it? In what time frame does this decision have to be made?

2. **Gathering information**

What do you need to know to make the decision? Who do you know who can help you understand how these decisions usually go? Are there professionals or experts who can help me understand the decision that needs to be made?

3. **Brainstorming alternatives**

What are my choices and options? Who can help me think out of the box?

4. **Assessing those alternatives**

If I try this choice on, how does it fit, how do I feel? What are the pros and cons of each of these? Which of these options align best with my values? What would I choose if the one choice I am attached to was taken off the table?

5. Taking action

Making a choice, finalizing the decision. Does this decision allow me to be the person I want to be one year from now? Three years from now? Five years from now?

Sounds simple, right? Not really, because, to further complicate the process, we all have different decision-making styles that have been developed over the years based on our own past experiences with making decisions.

Decision-Making Style Examples

A few examples of different decision-making styles include but are not limited to:

- **People who like to make decisions based on a majority and consensus after presenting alternatives / options to a group.**

"I am going to divorce my husband because my whole family believes I can do much better."

- **People who like to make decisions based upon information, data, numbers or research.**

"I am going to get divorced because over 50% of marriages end in failure, that's more than half, why bother."

- **Those that make decisions based on how they feel or what their instincts are telling them**.

"I am going to get divorced because my gut is telling me to, this just doesn't feel right."

- **People who only like to make decisions after compiling lists identifying the pros and cons of each choice.**

"I have decided to divorce my husband after making a list and there are more reasons to leave than stay."

Jeremy: What would you say is the best process or the best way for people to be involved in the process?

Tracy: I have seven steps that will help facilitate positive involvement in the decision-making process.

Seven Steps to Effective Divorce Decision-Making

Step #1: Breathe

First and foremost, the most important thing for people to do when making decisions in divorce is to breathe. Literally, take a deep breath and then take another. Give yourself some time. People tend to rush into the process so they can quickly move past the pain. By slowing down the decision-making process, you are able to more effectively develop and consider options, address emotional issues that may be barriers to the decision-making process, weigh and assess the best and worst case scenarios and determine true wants and needs, not just knee jerk reactions.

Step #2: Give Yourself a Break

The second thing to do in the process is to give yourself a break. Acknowledge that divorce is difficult. You are dealing with a lot of stuff at one time with a lot of feelings and emotions intertwined. These overwhelming feelings can make even the most rational person act and behave against their "Best

Self" and their own best interests. By becoming aware of the impact that these emotions are having, you can give yourself permission to seek out alternatives and support such as a thinking partner or divorce coach. These supports can help you process and sort through all of your feelings, allowing you the opportunity to identify potential outcomes and consequences of your decisions. You don't want to make emotional decisions in the short term that will have lasting impact well into the future.

Step #3: Identify What Decisions Need to be Made

The third important thing to do in the process is to identify what decisions need to be made. Clarity can often be obtained by stepping back from the process and looking at it from a distance rather than in the middle of it. By being clear and reasonable about what your priorities are and breaking down the pieces at hand, you will be able to more effectively engage in a decision-making process that is reflective of a positively manageable place rather than one filled with chaos and conflict. By identifying what decisions need to be made and prioritizing them one at a time, you can effectively manage the decision-making process without it becoming all consuming.

Step #4: Frame the Process and Issues

The fourth important thing to do is to frame the process and issues. The drama of divorce can cause people to be defined by the process. You do not want to become your own divorce story. It is important for you to decide who you want to be and how you want others to see you in the process so that your decisions align with your values. Additionally, by framing or putting the issues into context, you are able to deal with the real issues, not the perceived ones motivated out of fear, hate, anger, frustration or revenge.

Step #5: Identify and Find Professionals/Experts for Help, Support, and Advice as Needed

The fifth important step in the decision-making process is to identify and find professionals/experts for help, support, and advice as needed. In divorce, there is a lot of information you will need to gather so that you are able to make the best decisions possible for you and your family. Additionally, expert professionals may be able to identify potential options or alternatives that you may have never considered simply because you did not know. Professionals can help educate you on the process, guide, support and advise so that you are able to effectively engage in an informed decision-making process. Which professional or expert you seek should depend on what information or level of support you require. Some expert divorce professionals include, but are not limited to:

- family law attorneys

- Certified Divorce Coaches (CDC®)

- Certified Divorce Financial Analysts (CDFA®)

- therapists

Step #6: Test Out Your Decision Before Committing to Any Final Process

The sixth important step in the decision-making process is to test out your decision before committing to any final process. Try it out in a variety of different situations. You want to be able to look at the best and worst scenarios before making the decision final. You can involve others in this process as well by asking for feedback from someone who disagrees with your view or asking someone to shoot some holes into your ideas. Challenge yourself to walk down that path and see if you are comfortable with the reality. If so, then you can move forward with the decision. If there are questions or hesitation, you can go back to assessing other alternatives and options.

Step #7: Be Kind to Yourself

The seventh and last important step of the decision-making process is to be kind to yourself. There is no need to beat yourself up over a decision that you made that might not have been the best. It happens. Being able to step back and process without being overly critical of yourself is essential. Take what you learned from the experience as an opportunity to grow and proceed accordingly.

Jeremy: Would you say by taking action and engaging in an effective decision-making process, even if it's slowly, you have more of a feeling of confidence?

Tracy: Absolutely! No matter how small the decision was, YOU engaged in the process. YOU made a decision. YOU exerted your ability to take control during a time when you might have felt out of control or incapable. These small decision-making processes, building upon one another, inevitably give in return, confidence. It's like taking your first step. Once you take the first step, and you didn't fall down, no matter how small of a step it was, it gave you the confidence and excitement to take the next step. That's really what we call the process of self-empowerment. Taking charge of your own life, knowing and owning your power without giving it away. Telling yourself, "I got this, I can do this", as well as celebrating your successes.

Jeremy: Can you elaborate just a little bit on the process of self-empowerment. How would you define or what is self-empowerment?

Tracy: In the simplest form, self-empowerment is taking charge of your own life. If we were talking about Maslow's hierarchy of needs, self-empowerment would be equivalent to the very top of the hierarchy, "self-actualization". Maslow's Hierarchy of Needs model was built on the idea that people are motivated to achieve certain needs. When one need is fulfilled, a person seeks to fulfill the next one, and so on, climbing up the hierarchy. Self-actualization sits atop all the other levels of physiological needs, safety needs, love and belongingness and self-esteem needs. It is considered the highest level need. Self-actualization is about realizing one's personal potential, self-fulfillment, seeking personal growth and peak experiences.

Maslow's Hierarchy of Needs

In divorce, I often see clients who have lost their self-empowerment and their ability to achieve their need for self-actualization because they believe their other needs to be threatened. As such, that fear allows the divorce and the divorce process to define them and there is a loss. By taking charge and engaging in the decision-making process, you regain that control. Part of that self-actualization, that self-empowerment is having decision-making power of your own — to not let other people make the decisions for you. It is also important that your decisions be consistent with your core essence and values, authentic to who you are and who you choose to be.

As a mediator, I believe mediation to be an extremely self-empowering process for many individuals because they are the ones engaging in the decision-making process. They are the ones verbalizing for themselves

193 · TRACY CALLAHAN

what's important to them, their values and their decisions based on those values. It is a skill, and it is a negotiation, and it takes a certain level of confidence, for sure, but that's the ultimate step. Self-empowerment is achieved by engaging in a decision-making process and not having somebody else engage for you or not having a judge tell you what will happen in your divorce, what your family will look like in your divorce, what your assets and debts will look like in your divorce. Just you as a participant in the divorce realizing your own personal potential, deciding together with your spouse, what your life will look like moving forward.

Jeremy: Let's talk about the self-empowered decision-making process. How a self-empowered decision-making process takes one from action to agreement in the divorce process?

Tracy: By engaging in effective decision-making that is consistent with your values, personal interests, and authentic self, you are taking the action necessary to positively and amicably move towards an agreement in your divorce. A divorce is completed when a marital settlement agreement has been done, agreed upon and so ordered by the court. Self-empowered decision-making gets you from action to agreement by engaging in the process, identifying the issues, assessing alternatives and options, and making decisions as to how you, your spouse, and children will move forward, apart from the marriage. Through this self-empowered process, you can take action, minimize conflict and discord, and define how you want this to be and look in an amicable manner. Whether your goal is your divorce settlement agreement or an agreement with yourself as to how you are going to continue to proceed with your divorce, self-empowered decision-making is the action to get you there.

Jeremy: Can you share an example of a client that you worked with, some of the challenges they were going through, and how you helped them come to a resolution and overcome some common pitfalls?

Tracy: I had a client that came to me in the middle of her divorce process looking for help with decision-making. During her marriage of fifteen years, she had minimal to no dealings with the financial affairs of her household. Her husband handled all of the finances of the house and it was never a topic of discussion. She always had access to money for household expenses, children's expenses and her daily activities and never had reason to question any money matters. Although she had been financially independent prior to getting married and worked in marketing, she never enjoyed handling money and was happy to hand over the responsibility to her husband when she left her job shortly after getting married to start their family.

When she was confronted with the fact that her husband wanted to end their marriage and get divorced, she was completely immobilized by her fear of how she was going to manage. As a stay at home mom, with no knowledge of their finances, she was completely scared and overwhelmed. Shortly after announcing the divorce, her husband moved out of the home and she was left with a stack of bills and responsibilities for the financial management of their home that she had never had to deal with before.

This process for her was incredibly overwhelming. She was scared and didn't know where to begin or what to do. In our work together, we were able to sort out her concerns and deal with the emotional anguish of her situation. By engaging in a self-empowered decision-making process, she was able to effectively identify the financial issues, set goals, gather the information she needed from financial professionals, seek out alternatives and options, assess her options and then make decisions as to how she will proceed with handling the money. With little to no help from her husband, she was able to get organized and stable in a very short period of time.

More and more, she was able to make financial decisions confidently on her own. Even something as small as figuring out what the balance of the mortgage was and figuring out where the accounts were and making decisions on how she was going to handle them, empowered her. When the couple finally went to mediation to work on their settlement agreement, she was well equipped, confident and was behaving in a manner consistent with her values, best interests, the interests of her family and her identified "Best Self". Her husband was quite taken aback by her confidence, self-assurance and independence in the decision-making of their financial matters and as such, each played an equal and positive role in their settlement agreement.

Through the decision-making process, she was able to engage in a powerful place. The more she participated in the decision-making process, the easier it was for her to be able to come to a settlement agreement in which she felt confident. She felt the process was fair and there was less conflict than the numerous years of their marriage when she avoided it and did not engage in the process.

Jeremy: Any final words of advice? Is there one lesson you think that everybody should take away from this?

Tracy: That we can't control anybody's behavior, we can only control our reaction to their behavior. I say that in regards to everything from the divorce process to the decision-making process. We, as individuals, have an opportunity to define who we want to be in the process. We might not be able to control the situation, we might not be able to control somebody else's behavior, but we can take responsibility for ourselves and engage in a process that is consistent with our core essence and being.

Again, the whole concept of self-empowerment and self-actualization; where are you now, defining how you choose to behave in the divorce, how you choose to handle challenging situations, how you choose to be perceived by others and how you move forward apart from your marriage, is not dependent on what other people do or how they behave. We can only control ourselves. The more that we tap into what's important to us, who we are, who we'd like to be and not letting even something as difficult as divorce define that process for us, we're so much better off.

Jeremy: That's great advice. People often forget that we don't have control over other people's actions, but we have control over how we react to things.

Tracy: Definitely. That's really taking the high road in divorce. We can't control the divorce process, but, we can control how we handle it, how we perceive it, and how we engage in it — that's all part of self-empowered decision-making.

Jeremy: Thank you, Tracy. In conclusion, can you share with us how someone can learn more about your practice and get in touch with you?

Tracy: My practice is called Mediating-Matters and you can find me on Facebook at www.facebook.com/MediatingMatters and on Twitter as @MediatingMatter or, visit my website at www.mediating-matters.com.

Key Takeaways

√ Decision-making is a primary factor in the divorce process and can be greatly impacted by time, emotion, and change/transition.

√ Decisions that need to be made in divorce primarily fall into 3 main categories: parenting-visitation, asset/debt/property division, and financial support.

√ Decision-making is a cognitive process that requires one to: set goals, gather information, brainstorm options, assess options, and take action.

√ Engaging in a 7-Step Process to Effective Decision-Making will help facilitate positive involvement in the decision-making process.

√ Taking action and engaging in an effective decision-making process leads to self-empowerment and confidence.

√ By engaging in an effective decision-making process that is consistent with one's personal values, interests, and authentic self, one can positively successfully move to an agreement in their divorce.

ABOUT TRACY CALLAHAN, MA, CDC®

Tracy Callahan, MA, is an experienced mediator, serving families in the state of Florida as a Supreme Court of Florida Certified Family Mediator.

After starting her independent practice, Mediating-Matters, LLC in Palm Beach County, FL, Tracy recognized how very difficult the divorce process can be for all parties involved, especially those with children. As such, Ms. Callahan added Divorce Coaching to her practice and has been working as a Certified Divorce Coach in addition to her role as a family mediator. In her work, Ms. Callahan develops partnerships with her clients to empower them in managing their life transitions. Through supportive guidance and personal coaching, clients gain the clarity and confidence needed to reduce the overwhelm inherent in the divorce process and engage in a self-empowered decision-making process.

Ms. Callahan received her BS and her MA from New York University in the healthcare field and worked as a healthcare administrator and operations specialist for many years before joining the field of mediation and divorce.

Tracy is the proud mother of two teenage children and is passionate about her practice and the work she does with families in crises.

BUSINESS: Mediating-Matters, LLC

WEBSITE: www.mediating-matters.com

EMAIL: callahanmediating@gmail.com

PHONE: 866.506.5110

LOCATION: Juno Beach, FL

FACEBOOK: www.facebook.com/MediatingMatters

LINKEDIN: www.linkedin.com/in/tracy-callahan-7b598a57

TWITTER: @MediatingMatter

CHAPTER TEN

COLLABORATIVE DIVORCE – THE BIGGEST SECRET FOR ACCESS TO THE HIGH ROAD IN DIVORCE

Interview with **Kurt B. Chacon**, JD, CDC®

"Dismiss the inevitable and embrace the impossible." —
Kurt Chacon

Jeremy: Kurt, you have a unique background in that you've experienced family court as a family law attorney, as a parent going through a divorce, a divorce coach for the last five years, and as a collaborative law attorney.

Given that litigation can be so profitable, what inspired you to choose collaborative law and coaching instead of traditional family law?

Kurt: My experience in divorce includes three perspectives: as a child, as a parent, and as an attorney. My parents were divorced in the 1970's. Back then, few couples got divorced, and divorce was not seen as a problem. Consequently, the behavior of parents and the conflict that occurred in the legal system was likewise not considered significant. And no one talked about it. That experience of divorce was unnecessarily tragic, which is an observation made from hindsight.

When I realized I was going to divorce, I committed to choosing differently than my parents, striving to minimize the impact of the divorce on my children. My wife and I decided on collaborative divorce as our process. We each retained an attorney and both said they did collaborative work. I have come to learn not all lawyers embrace the collaborative process, and such was the case with ours. The method we used was NOT the process I have since studied and practiced. Based on that experience, and because I am passionate about the collaborative process, I have committed to it as an attorney and coach, continuing to improve my skills through training and experience, bringing expertise, experience and passion to my practice and clients. I want parents to have the option to divorce differently and with dignity and minimize the impact on their children.

Jeremy: How did these childhood experiences and other experiences shape your outlook on the divorce process?

Kurt: My parents' divorce directly impacted my life significantly and adversely. Children mirror what they see in their parents for good or bad, right or wrong. I experienced the worst of the worst. Without going into detail, my parents continued in conflict, bitterness, anger, blame, resentment with each other - and by extension me - for years to come. It took my divorce for me to realize fully the profound impact this experience had on me and my choices leading to my divorce

My parents were poor role models as a husband and a wife during marriage and as parents during divorce. Once my divorce was imminent, it was clear I had to make a different choice. I said to myself, "Okay. I'm going to choose something else going forward. I'm going to choose more cooperation. I'm going to choose forgiveness. I'm going to choose to let the past go." Not only was my divorce different than my parent's in a profoundly positive way, it empowered me to put that divorce experience from my past in the past and move forward differently, not only through my divorce but also in my life after divorce.

Jeremy: Many people certainly have these preconceived notions about the divorce process. They believe that they have to hire an attorney and go through the family court system.

Can you describe what the differences are between the collaborative law process and the more common litigious process?

Kurt: Every divorce requires a petition asking the court to grant a divorce, and every divorce ends with the judge signing a decree granting the divorce. Everything that happens between these points is completely different, depending upon the process you choose.

In the collaborative process, nothing occurs in court. The parties do everything according to a Collaborative Law Participation Agreement. And that is a private agreement. All the "discovery" -- the exchange of information between the parties to gather the facts-- takes places simply by request. If one party asks for something, the other party produces that document, or thing, or item -- because that is what they agreed to do and because the building of trust is important in the collaborative process. Virtually everything that happens in the process happens with the parties and the team in the same room together.

There is a team of professionals (depending on the jurisdiction) — lawyers, financial professionals, and/or mental health professionals — in the room at these meetings. They support the divorcing parties in several ways…

Collaborative Divorce Goals

- Discover and shape the interests and goals of the parties;

- Support the parties in understanding the current situation of the marriage, financial status of the marital estate, value of the assets of the marital estate, and custody, parenting time (possession) and support of any children;

- Engage and support the creation of different ideas, options, and proposed solutions;

- Measure those proposed solutions in light of the stated interest and goals of the parties;

- Ensure the proposed agreement functions as the parties intend and that all possibilities and contingencies are considered

The collaborative process is client-centered, meaning the clients control the pace of the process. In litigation, the process is judicially-centered. The court, the judge, and the lawyer determine the pace of the process.

The collaborative process is interest-based negotiation while litigation (and in most cases mediation) is position-based negotiation. Interests and positions are very different, and the process of negotiating each is different and can result in significantly more ill-will post-divorce between the parties.

The final and perhaps the most significant financial difference as I see it is the withdrawal provision of the Collaborative Law Participation Agreement (CLPA). In most jurisdictions, either party may opt out of the collaborative process. If so, the CLPA requires lawyers on both sides to withdraw from the case and clients must find new counsel to represent them in litigation. This is a huge financial incentive for the clients and the lawyers to stay in the collaborative process and reach an agreement. There is no incentive for lawyers or clients to "milk" the collaborative process then jump to litigation. That is huge.

Jeremy: That's an excellent point. Regarding building that trust, the exchange of information is much different than the litigious process where discovery can be almost a form of harassment, right? Such as asking for things like hard drives and anything that you can think of just to be more strategic and adversarial rather than building trust and more of a collaborative model.

Kurt: I agree with that. The discovery process can be used for any number of purposes not intended to move the case to resolution. Since about 95% of all divorce litigations settle out of court -- and to be clear, a settlement out of court is an agreement -- all of that information you just described has to be produced in a way that will allow it to be admissible at a trial that realistically will never happen.

That's a ninety-five percent chance that all the time and money the parties spent collecting this evidence in a court-admissible form will never be admitted to a court anywhere. But, they have paid --what I like to call the "litigation premium" -- for that versus simply coming to the table with all of their financial and other relevant information, exchanging it, and getting a complete, crystal clear picture of the marital estate, value of the assets, and parenting considerations. This can be done far more quickly than litigation discovery. You can spend up to 20 or 30 times more money and time on discovery in litigation for a trial that will probably never happen.

Jeremy: Right. With ninety-five percent of this evidence never being admitted to court, why start from the outset in an adversarial context? It doesn't make any sense.

Kurt: I agree with that. People hear the word "collaborative," and that's what they think, "We pretty much have to agree." Even lawyers will say, "Well, you pretty much have to be in agreement to go through the collaborative process." I can't stress this enough: no, you don't have to agree at any level to opt for a collaborative divorce. It's all about how you come to an agreement. If you choose litigation, do you think you come to the table agreeing? No - but there is a ninety-five percent chance you will agree!

That's going to be right on the courthouse steps before a judge takes what I like to call the "meat cleaver of justice" to your family and your estate. Clients agree rather than allowing and risking the judge deciding who gets what. This is how out-of-court settlements are done. "Well, if we don't take this today, the court may rule against us," and everybody gets anxious right at the end. Or "If we don't make/take this offer, it will be off the table tomorrow." (This is the absolute WORST time to make a decision of any significance - hastily, desperately, fearfully and without adequate time to think it over between reaching an agreement and actually signing off.)

Or, you can reach an agreement by sitting across the table from the only other person who cares about your children as much as you do, the only other person who knows the family as well as you do, the only other person who has as much invested in the outcome as you. The two people who have the most at stake create the agreement in their way and on their own time. The collaborative process lets the spouses literally "take the reins" of their divorce.

Jeremy: Those are excellent points, and you've underscored many of the benefits of collaborative law.

Can you crystallize or summarize what you see as the key advantages of collaborative law and collaborative divorce process vs. litigation?

Kurt: First of all, collaborative divorce will never be as inexpensive as sitting down at the kitchen table and coming to an agreement with your spouse. However, it will be cheaper than litigation for some of the reasons I've touched on previously.

Second, you keep everything private since you don't go to court.

Third, each person has a lawyer, and their incentive is to get you to an agreement. Everything is done by agreement, and in that way the parties build trust. Allegations are not made simply for the sake of leverage for more money or more parenting time. Mental health professionals and financial professionals in the collaborative process are neutral. They give you objective, neutral advice as you move forward. Neutral experts cost a lot less than a host of "dueling experts" hired specifically to attack the other spouse, their claims, and their experts.

The collaborative process is not about the past. It's about the present and the future. It helps people move away from what happened five years ago, or ten years ago, and moving forward to their new life. The collaborative process puts the two people who know the family best in charge of what happens. That, to me, is significant. If you have children and are concerned about the impact of divorce on your kids, choosing a collaborative divorce gives you the best chance to minimize that impact and walk away with a cooperative, cordial, supportive co-parenting relationship that will affect your children in a positive way going forward. It's not a guarantee. But it gives you a much better chance of doing that. I can tell you this from personal experience as well as professional observation.

Jeremy: Because it is a cooperative and collaborative process where an agreement is not forced down your throat, and you have time to review it, compliance is going to be much higher. The likelihood of going to court to solve every single dispute is going to be lessened.

Kurt: I like the way you said that. It makes your chances of ongoing cooperation much more likely. It's not a guarantee. It's much more likely. Having to sit across the table from your spouse and talk about options, and agreements, and so forth is a lot different than having your lawyer call their lawyer up and have a settlement negotiation where people don't have to see each other and can use lawyers as a go-between. It is much easier for someone to be difficult, bitter, spiteful, obstinate - take your pick - when your lawyers speak for you rather than sitting across the table from your spouse discussing options.

Jeremy: Exactly, because when you lose the discourse, now, you're relying on fighting through proxies.

Kurt: Correct, and the proxies sometimes don't get along. Yes, many times lawyers don't like each other. Sometimes, the lawyer(s) and the judge don't get along. These circumstances can drastically affect the pace, tone, and outcome of the process. At some point, the parties need to be in control, take back the reins from the judicial system and the lawyers, and make it a client-focused rather than judicially-focused process.

Jeremy: Great points on all fronts. Now, the terms "collaborative divorce" and "mediation," they're both misunderstood and sometimes, people think they're the same. Can you briefly explain what the difference is between a collaborative divorce and mediation?

Kurt: A mediator is someone who is trained in dispute resolution. Many times, in the family law courts, mediators have some depth of experience in family law. At some point, the judge will order mediation - not in every case but the vast majority. Parties meet with lawyers and a mediator to seek an agreement. Most of the process takes place in separate rooms. The mediator goes back and forth between rooms with potential settlement offers. The mediator sometimes points out where a client is being unrealistic versus what the court might do in the hopes of getting people to get to a point of agreement. They go back and forth and back and forth.

A lot of times, as the day wears on, people's nerves fray. Let's assume each lawyer is charging $500 an hour. You have a mediator charging $250 an hour. You've been there 8 hours, and that's ten grand, right? People get anxious about the amount of money being spent, worried about reaching - or not - an agreement, and many times, an agreement is entered into with pressure, anxiety, and undue haste at the end of a very long and contentious day. To quote a judge I know: a mediated settlement agreement is an agreement created by lawyers and approved by the client. There is an extensive body of law dealing with rushing to get these agreements "approved" by a court ASAP. Why? Because people go home, sleep on it, and wake up with an "OMG what have I done?" moment and they want out of the agreement. And rightly so. They recognize how hastily and desperately the agreement was created.

Mediation is sometimes used in the collaborative process to help clients get unstuck on a particular issue, but generally, mediation is considered part of the litigation process. Collaboratively trained mediators are skilled at getting clients to talk about what it is they want and why. In the collaborative process, there's no time pressure. We move at a much slower pace, giving everyone the opportunity to come to an agreement, think about it, ask more questions about it, understand its implications, tweak it, and move forward.

Collaborative agreements are agreements that are created by clients and approved by the lawyers. The lawyers are there to make sure that what the clients agreed to can manifest itself in reality when the divorce is final. "You want this to happen; we have to have this structure in place. You want that to happen; we have to have these things in place to make sure it gets done, and it's legal, and if it isn't done, we have recourse." The collaborative process allows the clients to be in control. The mediated process is virtually none of those.

Jeremy: Now, also within collaborative law, we hear the terms "interest-based negotiation," "client-centered process." What exactly do those mean?

Kurt: In litigation, the process is judicially-centered. Local and state rules of procedure, the particular court calendar and the schedule of the lawyers dictate the pace of what happens. Yes, occasionally, a client might get asked about their availability on a particular date, but everything is going to happen according to the court's calendar and when the lawyers could be there, or not. That doesn't occur in collaborative law. That's what I call being client-centered versus judicially-centered.

A client-centered process means the clients control the pace of what happens. In the collaborative process, since everything takes place out of court and most everything happens at client meetings, the clients can go at a pace that works for them. They can go much faster than things might go in court, or they can go a bit more slowly, or whatever works for them. The clients have the reins.

What is the difference between interest-based negotiation vs. position-based negotiation? Well, for example, an interest of a parent entering divorce might be to maintain a close and loving relationship with their children. A position of a parent might be seeking full custody of the children. There are limitless possibilities that further that interest, but there is only one outcome that supports the position of sole custody of the children post-divorce. Collaborative professionals are trained to help identify interests. Many times there are common interests and there can be a win/win. That's not what happens in litigation. In litigation lawyers negotiate from positions, as in "I win, you lose." The process is focused on wanting to get the most. The collaborative process is focused on getting what clients most want.

Jeremy: You touched on this before, but I think it warrants going into more detail. There is a misconception that clients need to be agreeable before they go through the process, but that's not necessarily the case. Can you expound on that?

Kurt: I will say that since the clients will be sitting in the same room that at least they need to be able to be civil to each other. They need to be able to have open and honest communication. That's why the team of lawyers, the mental health professional, the financial professional is put in place. The lawyers are advocates; the others are neutrals. Neutrals do not have an advocate relationship with a particular client. They do not take a particular stand for what either client hopes to gain, proposes or seeks. Within the process and with the support of the team, clients reach an agreement.

In litigation, the solutions to disagreements are generally focused on what the court will and won't do. And the solutions are based on "standard this, standard that" because that's what courts and judges do. That is "spotlight thinking", seeing too few solutions without time to consider anything else. And spotlight thinking leads to poor decision-making.

The collaborative process is completely different than that. In the collaborative process, anything and everything that might solve the problems is available. In the end, everybody comes to an agreement. Everyone has time to examine near limitless options with enough time to reflect and make good decisions. It's just a way of taking the reins back from the court and the lawyers, and keeping the decision-making process and the pace of that in control of the two people who know the marriage and the children best - the spouses.

Jeremy: I find it a funny too regarding the misconception about being agreeable because you think a litigious process such as family court is going to make you more agreeable or less agreeable.

Kurt: Exactly. Litigation doesn't necessarily make you more agreeable. But I can tell you this: that process can poison the well going forward for any relationship between the parties, during and after litigation, especially if they have children to the point that parents refuse to attend children's events because of anger and resentment toward the other parent. God forbid somebody showed up at a sports game with a new relationship interest during the litigation process. Then it's "on like Donkey Kong" at that point in the litigation - more money for the lawyers! In addition, there are holidays, graduations, weddings, all the things that we as parents hope to enjoy with our children in their lives going forward. Those priceless moments can either be pleasant and joyful for everyone, or they can be a beat down, especially for the children because they suffer the most so the parents can wallow in bitterness. How you choose to reach an agreement can affect children going forward until whichever parent passes first.

Jeremy: Right. That's a huge point that can't be emphasized enough.

You had mentioned the privacy involved in a collaborative process where each party is trying to cooperate. In an adversarial process like family court, it can be a place where potentially nasty allegations can be introduced, that damage and the resentment it breeds is hard to take back.

You can start in collaboration or a collaborative process, and then go to litigation as a worst case scenario, but once you have planted your feet in the ground and you've already started from an adversarial posture, it's much harder to undo the damage that's already been done.

Would you agree with that?

Kurt: I would agree with that. Now, sometimes, that can be done by the personality between the lawyers and the judge, and sometimes, we have had cases in which people have opted into the collaborative process and out of litigation, and then the minute the parties took back the reins of communication, the case settled, but you're exactly right. The allegations that are sometimes made, and how they're made, and how they are received by the parties can make people bitter going forward.

Research has been done. People have been interviewed ten to fifteen years after their divorce in which they got a good deal, and they're not happy. The reason they're not happy is because of the process. While they may have gotten a good deal from a lawyer's point of view, they did not get a good deal from their own point of view (years later) because no one sat down with them and explored really what they were genuinely interested in and what was most important to them.

In litigation, I've had people come in and say, "I want to minimize the impact of divorce on my children," and turned right around and said, "I don't want my spouse to get a dime. I want all the money. As far as I'm concerned, they can live in a 1-bedroom apartment and drive a Ford Pinto." Sometimes, you have to sit back, and scratch your head and say, "Well, okay. How exactly does that minimize the impact of divorce on the children if they feel like one of their parents is broke and a deadbeat?" Take it from me: children want their parents to be happy after divorce and to prosper. They want what is best for both parents and seeing one parent prospering at the expense of the other is seen as unfair.

In the collaborative process, if a client says he/she has an interest or goal in minimizing the impact of divorce on the children, then everything a client does, says, suggests or proposes, is measured against that stated interest. Is the behavior, proposal, etc. furthering their stated interest, or working against it? Lawyers rarely explore interests of clients in litigation, much less ask questions about how the process is meeting those interests. However, we do explore the interests of clients in the collaborative process.

Jeremy: It's almost like the psychological term, "behavioral interviewing," and aligning one's goals with their present actions.

In the family court law process, an attorney may think more conflict equates to more money.

Kurt: People need to understand that. In litigation, lawyers may not think more fighting is wise, but they will gladly take fees associated with mindless arguing and an unwillingness to reach an agreement. They have no real incentive to stop it, and every incentive to allow it to continue. In the collaborative process, open communication and movement toward resolution are what the team seeks. They don't have an incentive to milk the process and then jump into litigation because they can't profit from it.

That is a huge difference and one which clients should consider when choosing a process for divorce: what incentives or disincentives do lawyers have in a process to protect my interests?

Jeremy: Now, what would you say are some of the most common obstacles or misconceptions that people face when they're considering divorce?

Kurt: One significant misconception is thinking the judge has the wisdom of Solomon, and will see the righteousness and truth of their position and see the wickedness of their spouse's lies. Judges are human and make decisions on their own personal views and beliefs. Nothing against judges, just a reality check. As we discussed, ninety-five percent of cases do not go before the judge for a trial, and the reality is the judge may never hear from either party directly, ever. Another misconception: the judicial process is not what people think it is. People think they are joining a client-centered process, not realizing they're not the boss of anything. The court and the lawyers control everything. Many clients cannot can't get on board with the process they've chosen. They choose this process not really knowing they have other options. Instead, they opt for a process that leaves them with the control of only one thing: "Yes, I'll take that" or "No, I won't." Who would sign up for that if there is another option?

People think that their lawyer will work closely with them, and they'll have this great relationship, and their lawyer will protect their interests. That happens less frequently than you'd think. The reality is litigators almost never identify a client's actual interests, but rather negotiate and do battle over positions, seeking to get the most. That is why research shows clients who get the most are rarely happy about it.

A major obstacle is extreme emotions, which result in all-or-nothing thinking and a "my way or the highway" negotiating style which leads nowhere. And the reality clients seem to miss, and lawyers and judges are very good at ignoring, is that the spouses are the real decision makers. Spouses can take back the reins of their divorce for the sake of both their financial future and the future of their children by opting OUT of litigation. That is exactly what collaborative divorce does for the client - it puts the two people who know what is best, in charge.

Jeremy: Going back to your first point, people often confuse legal justice with fairness.

Kurt: Exactly. For example, a client goes to a hearing for temporary orders. "What are we going to put in place regarding child support, visitation, and income, before we can get to a point where we can get a trial or settle this?" In Dallas County, for example, you have 20 minutes in front of the judge. You don't get to have half a day for a judge to "see your truth". You get 20 minutes for the judge to hear your plea for justice. If you're having a bad day for whatever reason, guess what? You are stuck with a bad result until your case goes to trial and you can change the judge's mind - NOT. That temporary hearing might be the last time you see that judge, and you had a bad day.

Jeremy: It's like going through the drive-through at McDonald's! But, instead of picking up a "Happy Meal," you're relying on a judge to make a decision that could impact your life and your children's lives!

Clearly, compared to litigation, there are so many more advantages to the collaborative divorce process. Why do you think collaborative divorce isn't more widespread?

Kurt: Four reasons: 1. Not knowing about it. 2. Not asking about your options. 3. Not being told about it. 4. Being told it isn't right for you.

First, most people outside the legal profession do not know about it, so they do not know to even ask about it. Also, clients almost never ask for alternatives to litigation, so none are even discussed. If clients have heard about collaborative divorce and ask a lawyer about it (and the lawyer is not a skilled practitioner of it) that lawyer is likely to say, "It's not right for you." And we can circle back to the idea that people, including lawyers, think spouses have to be in agreement to choose a collaborative divorce.

Many times lawyers won't even tell a client there are other options. The legal profession is debating whether it is unethical NOT to discuss all options with a client, including collaborative options.

Here is a "bonus" reason collaborative divorce is not more widespread: Divorce is over a fifty billion-dollar per year industry in this country. Lawyers want their piece of it. When a lawyer sees spouses who have sufficient assets to fund a divorce, it is easy to understand why lawyers not trained and committed to collaborative principles would either not mention collaborative or agree to the collaborative process despite not having the depth of training or passion for it. As a result, clients have a bad experience. And they tell everyone they know about it.

Jeremy: It seems odd that we replicated an adversarial model that might be suitable for criminal cases or business disputes, but can cause families considerable unnecessary trauma. And, this is the default process for families going through a transition or crisis?

Kurt: Yes. If you look at the family code in Texas, for instance, in the 1950's, the amount of pages and the number of words versus what it is now, you will understand the significance of the problem. The Family Code of Texas is under continuous revision. The legislature adds and amends provision after provision in an attempt to solve another problem. That usually creates one more issue for spouses to argue over, one more thing the judge gets to decide, and one more point for lawyers to get paid to argue.

Jeremy: Right. You solve one problem while creating ten more. It's the law of unintended consequences.

Kurt: Exactly. The more issues the family code tries to solve, the more people want to argue over them. And I'm not sure how we get past that other than seek new ways of reaching agreements.

Jeremy: Are there any couples that you'd say are not necessarily good candidates for the collaborative process?

Kurt: I will say there are some cases of abuse where perhaps the gravity and power of the judge and the legal system benefit the party victimized by abuse. Or, if there is such a tremendous disparity in the bargaining power between the couple, perhaps traditional litigation might be better because they can't be in the same room and communicate and negotiate as equals. Some people are simply high conflict and cannot ever engage in collaboration. They may not be good candidates.

Also, collaborative divorce is not about the past. If you are one who wants to seek retribution and revenge, this process is not for you. Collaborative is about the present and the future. If the past is where you want to live, then you need to go to litigation. That's going to serve you at least in the short-term. You most likely won't ever find the revenge or retribution you seek, probably because you'll run out of money, but you can certainly try and get even in litigation. A client can be an insensitive, uncooperative, uncommunicative, and unreasonable jerk, and play that out to the hilt in litigation.

I will also say that in each of those scenarios, many clients have successfully resolved their divorce through the collaborative process with the help of a great team.

Jeremy: Although a counter to that is that if there is a significant power imbalance, litigation can magnify the power imbalance because the party who has a controlling personality, may have the money, and they're going to fight, and leverage those attorneys.

Kurt: Right. It certainly can. Many times, the spouse that didn't make the money has to go to court to seek to get attorney's fees paid, temporary support, and the like. There are some people for whom litigation is the only way to move forward because of a power imbalance. But I believe with a good team of lawyers and professionals around both parties, a lot of great results can happen, even when the parties seemed very far apart or had a perceived power imbalance going in.

I tell people the collaborative process is not easy, and the reason it's not easy is because like you said, you don't talk through proxies, you can't throw it in the lap of the judge later on down the road. You don't have a lawyer telling you "you better take this". You have to sit across from your spouse and either make or take a deal you both create. And while that is the hard part, it is also the great part. The great part is you two are the ones making the decision. The two people who know what is best and have the most at stake make all the decisions.

Collaborative divorce is about the present and the future, and who the parents will be going forward, and whether or not parents will be good co-parents for their children and be a champion for your children at a time when they are most vulnerable.

I also say it's always cheaper to sit down at the kitchen table and come to an agreement. A collaborative divorce will never be cheaper than that, but it will be much less expensive than litigation when you consider the cost of discovery and hiring dueling experts.

I also tell clients collaborative divorce is not about what's fair. It's about what's acceptable. Each person has their own view of fairness and what is fair to one is seen as unfair to another, particularly when they are dividing one, finite pie, so to speak. Collaborative lawyers debate whether or not we should tell people that fairness doesn't matter. I say what we do is help people see "fairness" differently, more broadly and in light of their actual interests.

In the collaborative process, no one forces you to take an agreement, nobody is telling you, "you really need to take this." There is no fear of what the judge might do. In the end, that agreement is one that you chose freely to make, and it was acceptable to you. There are times when I look at my divorce decree and think, "That's an agreement that I chose. Nobody forced me to do it. There was not a judge threatening me that he was going to decide something. There was no mediator pressuring me. My lawyer was not pressuring me. I chose that agreement. It was acceptable." I look at it and say "Okay. I'm good with that." There is a sense of peace and satisfaction I get from that. I did not allow people who don't know my family and genuinely care about my family make any decisions about my family.

Jeremy: In general, in any divorce case, it's important that you hire the right professional.

Can you go into exactly what sort of criteria a person should use to evaluate and select a collaborative law attorney?

Three Criteria to Evaluate a Collaborative Law Attorney

Kurt: I would say three things…

1. **Experience**

One, their experience in the collaborative process. There are a lot of lawyers who've done their own collaborative divorce, and they, like myself, understand what a client goes through.

2. Training

Second, you want to know how much training a lawyer has had in collaborative processes and collaborative theory. You can examine that. You can ask them. They probably have a bio. You want somebody who has done the training and understood the process.

3. Commitment

Finally, commitment. Even though a lawyer may have handled some collaborative divorce cases and maybe had some training in it, but that's not what they embrace. They may not fully commit to the process. It is simply another revenue stream for them. They see a client with sufficient resources to pay the fee and do not want to let that kind of client walk out the door. That is what happened to me and my wife. And that is why I do this now. You should look for a lawyer that is all in.

Jeremy: Kurt, if someone is considering divorce, what are the top things they should focus on?

Top Five Tips When Considering Divorce

Kurt: Anyone considering divorce should focus on these 5 things.

1. Put a great team of people in place.

This could involve professionals from the legal, financial, mental health (adult and child) and spiritual fields — all of whom are committed to healthy divorce principles.

2. Be your best self and become self-aware.

Moving through divorce in a healthy way requires being the best we can be and being aware of what takes away from our best and recognizing when we are NOT at our best.

3. Attain knowledge.

Knowledge of the divorce process, all available options and alternatives, understanding what is at stake, and awareness of all decision points and outcomes, and knowing the difference between interests and goals vs. positions and entitlements.

4. Self-care and self-responsibility.

Knowing how to take care of yourself at a difficult time so you can be at your best (and make the best decisions) is crucial. Also, being responsible and accountable for your words and actions builds trust with others and integrity of self.

5. Forward thinking.

Acting as though you wish to be remembered for how you moved through this difficult time. Being a hero for others in the same place and a champion for those who depend on you.

These are the things I focus on with clients considering divorce. The biggest mistake people can make is NOT having these in place until it is too late — or not at all. I urge people to understand these five foundations BEFORE initiating divorce. Many times people discover divorce is NOT for them at this time — or ever. My passion is to help you identify the right choice for you.

Jeremy: Thanks so much, Kurt. Those were some great perspectives. In closing, how can someone learn more about you and your practice?

Kurt: I can be reached at www.divorcedifferently.org or on Facebook at www.facebook.com/divorcedifferntly.

Key Takeaways

√ **Collaborative divorce is simply a different way of reaching an agreement with your spouse, which you will do in 95% of all cases, even litigation.**

√ **Collaborative divorce is interest-based and client-centered, meaning you and your spouse control the speed and expense of the process, and use a team of professionals to find the win/win!**

√ **Many lawyers will not discuss collaborative divorce unless you ask them about it. Be sure to discuss collaborative divorce with more than one lawyer before choosing a process.**

√ **Collaborative divorce is not easy, it is not the least expensive, but it is about reaching an acceptable agreement, and it is about the future, not the past.**

√ **How parents behave during and after divorce have the greatest impact on how the divorce affects children. Collaborative divorce offers the best chance for you and your spouse to have a cordial, cooperative and supportive co-parenting relationship going forward.**

If you are considering divorce or know someone who is, please go to my website: www.divorcedifferently.org/freereport and download, "The Ten Things You MUST Know Before Seeking Divorce." This free report is essential to understanding divorce — whether you should or shouldn't, understanding all options and alternatives, the personal, professional and financial pitfalls to avoid, anticipating decision points and choices, understanding lawyers and the judicial processes, negotiation styles, and much more.

One again, this is a FREE report, and there is no obligation, no credit card, no subscription — just invaluable free information. Go to www. divorcedifferently.org/freereport get "The Ten Things You MUST Know Before Seeking Divorce."

ABOUT KURT B. CHACON, J.D., CDC Certified Divorce Coach®

Kurt B. Chacon is a Texas lawyer practicing collaborative divorce. He is a member of the State Bar of Texas, Collaborative Divorce Texas, and the Family Law and Collaborative Law sections of the State Bar of Texas, and the Denton County Collaborative Professionals. He is also a CDC Certified Divorce Coach®.

As a collaborative divorce attorney and a divorce coach, Kurt helps clients divorce differently and with dignity. Kurt's clients benefit from his experience of divorce both as a child and as a parent, as a client of the collaborative divorce process, as well as his observations as a divorce lawyer.

He lives in Dallas, Texas with his two children. He is a commissioned Stephen's Minister.

Building Heroes and Champions in the Midst of Life's Darkest Times.

BUSINESS: Divorce Differently

WEBSITE: www.DivorceDifferently.org

EMAIL: coachkurt@me.com

PHONE: 214.533.2634

LOCATION: Dallas, TX

FACEBOOK: www.facebook.com/divorcedifferntly

LINKEDIN: www.linkedin.com/in/kurt-chacon-72640b38

TWITTER: @divorcedffrntly

YOUTUBE:

www.youtube.com/channel/UCzdTWTJVW5Lkcc1N9enScMQ

Manufactured by Amazon.ca
Bolton, ON

18910464R00127